By bringing together Wesley's concern for the renewal of the heart and recent emotion theory, Clapper offers a bold vision for the church. He gives an account of how thinking, feeling, and acting belong together in who we are before God, then he calls the church to consider its role in shaping believers in all these dimensions. This book is a valuable resource for all who take John Wesley as a guide for their ministry.

—Sarah Heaner Lancaster
Methodist Theological School in Ohio

At last-a thoughtful and accessible account of Wesley's theology that addresses the central challenge of the church in our day as in his: the re-ordering of our loves. Clapper provides a much-needed voice of challenge to those who would dismiss the affectional ground of Christian faith or take it captive for non-Gospel purposes. In the end, the reader will find help and encouragement to *be* a Christian in all of living.

—Douglas S. Hardy
Nazarene Theological Seminary

The Renewal of the Heart
Is the Mission of the Church

The Renewal of the Heart
Is the Mission of the Church

Wesley's Heart Religion in the Twenty-First Century

GREGORY S. CLAPPER

CASCADE *Books* • Eugene, Oregon

THE RENEWAL OF THE HEART IS THE MISSION OF THE CHURCH
Wesley's Heart Religion in the Twenty-First Century

Cascade Books
A Division of Wipf and Stock Publishers
199 W. 8th Ave., Suite 3
Eugene, OR 97401

www.wipfandstock.com

ISBN 13: 978-1-60608-542-4

Cataloging-in-Publication data:

Clapper, Gregory Scott.

   The renewal of the heart is the mission of the church : Wesley's heart religion in the twenty-first century / Gregory S. Clapper.

   x + 150 p. ; 23 cm. Includes bibliographical references and index(es).

   ISBN 13: 978-1-60608-542-4

   1. Methodist Church—Doctrines. 2. Wesley, John, 1703–1791. 3. Emotions. I. Title.

BX8331.3 .C53 2010

Manufactured in the U.S.A.

To Georgia A. Rigg

Contents

Acknowledgments ix

Part I   **"Heart Religion" in Wesley's Own Voice**

1   Not *"What* Is Christianity?" but *"Who* Is a Christian?" 3

2   Wesley and Scripture on the Heart and its Renewal 17

Part II   **Wesley's "Heart Religion" Meets Twenty-First-Century Emotion Theory**

3   Overcoming the Obstacles to Hearing Wesley's Voice Today 33

4   Why Depth of Emotion Is not the Same as Intensity of Feeling 52

5   Wesley's *Orthokardia*: The Genesis and *Telos* of the Affections 68

Part III   **The Joyful Work of Heart Renewal Today**

6   Teaching for the Renewal of the Heart 91

7   Renewing the Heart through Preaching, Counseling, and Evangelism 107

Bibliography 133

Index 233

Acknowledgments

While much of this material appears in print for the first time here, parts appeared first in papers I have delivered at the national meetings of the American Academy of Religion, the Society for the Study of Wesleyan Psychology and Theology, the Wesleyan Philosophical Society, and the Oxford Institute of Methodist Theological Studies. I have also drawn on my writing as it appeared in the *Wesleyan Theological Journal*, *Methodist History*, and as chapters in four different volumes: *The Wesleyan Tradition: A Paradigm for Renewal* edited by Paul Chilcote (Abingdon Press, 2002), *Conversion in the Wesleyan Tradition* edited by Ken Collins and J. H. Tyson (Abingdon Press, 2001), *"Heart Religion" in the Methodist Tradition and Related Movements* edited by Richard Steele (Scarecrow Press, 2001), and *The Many Facets of Love: Philosophical Explorations*, edited by Thomas Jay Oord (Cambridge Scholars Publishing, 2007). Some material here also first appeared in my *John Wesley on Religious Affections* (Scarecrow Press, 1989). In the last chapter, I have employed some concepts and illustrations that received more in-depth treatment in my three books for Upper Room Books: *As if the Heart Mattered* (1997); *When the World Breaks your Heart* (1999) and *Living Your Heart's Desire* (2005).

The students in my classes on Wesley and Methodism at Christian Theological Seminary provided me stimulation and helpful feedback on this text, and I thank them for that. Special thanks to Robert Roberts of Baylor University who has helped me avoid misinterpreting his views in this text and, more generally, has helped my intellectual development through his writings over the past twenty years. My recently retired mentor at Emory University, Don Saliers, has continued to influence me through echoes from his seminar on "Passions, Emotions and Feelings," as well as his writings and his friendship. Special thanks to Jenna Staples who provided invaluable technical assistance in formatting much of my research for this book.

Being around people with well-formed hearts is perhaps the best way to understand what they look like in real life. In that, I have been most fortunate in being married to Jody. In appreciation for all who formed her heart, I dedicate this to the person most influential in that task, her mother, Georgia A. Rigg.

PART I

"Heart Religion" in Wesley's Own Voice

1 Not *"What* Is Christianity?" but *"Who* Is a Christian?"

Anyone who reads the works of John Wesley will immediately be struck with how often he refers to the "heart" or the "affections" or the "tempers." As we will see, this language is not dispensable rhetorical ornamentation, nor is it a reflection of an unsophisticated thinker who is pandering to the masses. For Wesley, one cannot make sense of Christianity without using the vocabulary of the heart.

Note well, though, that Wesley sees the gospel as something indisputably "objective" that comes from outside of us as "good news." We do not intuit the word of salvation through Christ by introspection or speculation; it comes to us as a proclamation. However, if our life is not marked by very specific and complex patterns of heart-response to that gospel, we have not really heard or understood the good news. Those patterns of response are what Wesley termed the religious "affections" or "tempers" of the heart.

Because of his emphasis on these patterns of response, Wesley is sometimes viewed as a kind of "pietist." This term is often used to indicate a kind of extreme emphasis on the "inner" life, and the "pietist" movement is typically explained away in the broad sweep of church-history generalizations as a narrow, historically located over-reaction to the excesses of the preceding era of arid, intellectual hair-splitting known as Protestant scholasticism. Even in our own time, when someone is so caught up with their own experience or prayer life that they uncritically accept any feeling or twinge as a "leading" of the Spirit—and, hence, an unquestionable road sign to Reality—they are often characterized as a "pietist." That characterization, then, is one that invites dismissal, not any serious attempt at appreciation.

I am not interested in analyzing "Pietism" in general, though there are several careful studies of particular individuals often called Pietists, and these studies can lead to a deeper and subtler appreciation of their thought.[1] Here I am interested specifically in examining the thought of John Wesley. Whether what I have to say about Wesley's understanding of the proper role of experience and emotion in the Christian life can be applied to other so-called Pietists, I will leave to others to judge. What is clear to me, though, is that what passes for the caricature of Pietism that I described above does not at all do justice to Wesley's vision of Christianity, and that Wesley's vision holds powerful possibilities for us still today— possibilities that contemporary emotion theory can help us see.

What Was Essential to Christianity for John Wesley?

It is clear that what was essential to Christianity according to Wesley was a life marked by the "religious affections." This life was made possible by, among other things, both an indispensable kernel of Christian doctrine, and, equally important, a particular *mode* of describing and expressing this doctrine. When trying to understand, or embody, Wesley's vision, the medium and the message must be completely integrated or Wesley's paradigm is violated.

John Wesley summarized his essential doctrines in slightly different ways at different times in his career, but there is enough consistency in these various summaries to detect a clear pattern. Three leading interpreters of Wesley's theology, Richard P. Heitzenrater,[2] Albert C. Outler,[3] and

---

1. See, for instance, the volumes in the series "Pietist and Wesleyan Studies" edited by Steve O'Malley and David Bundy published by Scarecrow Press.

2. See his *Wesley and the People Called Methodists*, where he discusses the different summaries: on 156 he quotes the "Principle of a Methodist" passage reproduced below; on 204 he mentions Wesley slightly different summary in a letter (*The Bicentennial Edition of Wesley's Works*, hereafter *Works*, 4:146) of "original sin, justification by faith and holiness consequent thereon"; on 214–15, quoting from Wesley's Journal and Diary (*Works*, 21:485) the three are referred to as "original sin and justification by faith, producing inward and outward holiness." On page 242, quoting Wesley's sermon at the funeral of George Whitefield (*Works*, 2:343), Heitzenrater lists the grand doctrines as "the new birth and justification by faith."

3. See his collected works, *The Albert Outler Library*, 1:258ff; 2:240ff; 3:422–47.

Thomas A. Langford,[4] have each taken Wesley's statement of his "main doctrines" in *Principles of a Methodist Farther Explained* as a representative summary.[5] In that piece, Wesley names the three essential doctrines that describe the doctrinal kernel of Christianity.

> Our main doctrines, which include all the rest, are three—that of repentance, of faith, and of holiness. The first of these we account, as it were, the porch of religion; the next, the door; the third, religion itself.[6]

There are several remarkable things about this statement, and I have commented on this doctrinal summary extensively in my book *As If the Heart Mattered: A Wesleyan Spirituality* (which makes the case for taking a specifically *theological*, rather than a purely psychological, grounding for spirituality). The part of this passage that I want to focus on here, however, is Wesley's descriptions of "repentance," "faith" and "holiness" as "*doctrines.*" To say that these three terms are, in and of themselves,

---

4. Langford, *Methodist Theology*, 7.

5. Randy Maddox in his "Vital Orthodoxy," says: "But the four doctrines that were mentioned far more often than any others were 1) original sin, 2) justification by faith, 3) the new birth and 4) holiness of heart and life" (10). Maddox's note to this passage refers to four different references in Wesley's works, which might lead the reader to think that this list of four doctrines is found in each of these passages, but that is not the case. For instance, in the reference to Wesley's sermon on the death of George Whitefield (Sermon 53, 341) Wesley simply refers to "the grand scriptural doctrines" without listing them. Two pages later in this sermon, Wesley does, as Heitzenrater pointed out (see note 2 above), summarize the "fundamental doctrines" in "two words—the new birth and justification by faith," (343) not the four-fold list seemingly implied by Maddox. Similarly, Maddox's reference to Wesley's sermon "On God's Vineyard" (Sermon 107, 516) yields this quote: "Were not the fundamental doctrines both of free, full, present justification delivered to you, as well as sanctification, both gradual and instantaneous? Was not every branch both of inward and outward holiness clearly opened and earnestly applied?" Again we do not see the fourfold listing. A charitable reading of Maddox here would have him mean that *taken as a sum*, the quotes in his references yield the four doctrines that are central to Wesley, but I think the weight of scholarly opinion makes Wesley's doctrinal summary in *Principles of a Methodist Farther Explained* to be the best single summary of what Wesley held to be central. Oddly, Maddox never refers to that piece in this article, nor in an even more recent summative look at Wesley's legacy: "'Celebrating the Whole Wesley' A Legacy for Contemporary Wesleyans." In my reading, original sin is addressed when unpacking the "porch of repentance," while justification, the new birth and holiness of heart and life are seen during elaborations of the "door of faith" and "the house itself." See chapters 2–4 in my *As If the Heart Mattered*.

6. *Works*, 9:227.

"doctrines" is, I think, more than a kind of lazy shorthand on the part of Wesley. This "doctrinal" summary speaks directly to what Wesley held to be most crucial in the whole Christian enterprise—namely, lived Christianity, describable in terms of the affections or tempers of the heart. Wesley's "main doctrines"—the indispensable components of essential Christianity—were best understood as they were enacted in human lives.

Now, as will be made clear in chapter 4 below, Wesley understood repentance, faith, and holiness as more than, and distinguishable from, feelings. Repentance, faith, and holiness are cognitive/affective embodiments of the Christian gospel experienced by Christian believers. Without these experiences, one might *know* all sorts of things *about* Christianity, and yet not *be* a real, fully mature Christian. However, while they are more than passing sensations, these embodiments of Christian truth clearly represent a different way of viewing "doctrines" than is more usual in the wider tradition.

Ted Campbell, in two papers he delivered earlier during the tercentenary year of Wesley's birth, makes an interesting distinction between two different lists of essential doctrines in Wesley's thought. One list of doctrines contains those that Campbell sees as essential "Christian" doctrines that all Christians believed, with a second list that was distinctive to the evangelical movement—those that were "distinctively Methodist." It is the three doctrines listed above—repentance, faith, and holiness—that make up the list of these distinctively Methodist doctrines. Campbell goes on to make the historical and liturgical point that these three doctrines can be seen in the very structure of a variety of Methodist hymnals going back to the time of John and Charles.[7]

What Campbell does not note, however, is that these three doctrines are key not only, or even primarily, because they are "distinctively Methodist" (the point that Lawrence Meredith makes with regard to these doctrines[8]), but because they are *most important for the foundational for-*

7. Campbell's papers delivered at the Manchester Wesley Tercentenary Conference, June 18, 2003, and at "The Legacy of John Wesley for the Twenty-First Century" conference, held at Asbury Theological Seminary, October 1–3, 2003. The larger list of Christian doctrines includes such standard tenets as the Trinity, the incarnation, etc. On this topic, see also Campbell's *Methodist Doctrine*, 19–20 and 31–33.

8. Meredith, "Essential Doctrine in the Theology of John Wesley."

mation of disciples. Because they are *indispensably formative of the heart* is most likely the reason they *became* distinctively Methodist. It is not their capacity to serve as denominational markers—their sociological "distinctiveness"—that makes them important, it is their formative capacity. They are the most important—or essential—"doctrines" because they shape the heart—they plug into (and/or create) the emotional capacities that Wesley saw as indispensable for being a Christian.

Typically, when the tradition speaks of these experiences with regard to "doctrine," we find discussions about "the doctrine of sin," or "the doctrine of justification by grace through faith," or "the doctrine of sanctification," and occasionally Wesley himself would use this kind of language.[9] These latter, traditional formulations of "doctrine" have one thing in common, though—they are abstract, secondary reflections on the primary lived realities that Wesley referred to by the terms "repentance," "faith," and "holiness." A life marked by these doctrine-shaped experiences will be a life marked by the religious affections—the signs of the renewed heart in the believer.

In order to see in more detail Wesley's theological vision and how it manifested itself in all of his published works, I want now to look at several specific ways that Wesley described the essence of Christianity, looking especially at his Sermons and his *Notes* on Scripture.

True Christianity in Wesley's Publications

The first sermon in the extant published corpus of Wesley's sermons is "Salvation by Faith," and by putting it first Wesley was making a clear statement that the will-mysticism of Law, Taylor, and Kempis—emphasizing our own disciplined efforts at spiritual growth—while useful, was not sufficient to salvation. He had rediscovered, both in his Aldersgate experience and in his studies of the *Homilies* and "Articles of Religion" of his church, that it is grace through *faith* that justifies us. The whole sermon is an exposition of what this faith is.

First of all, Wesley wants to make clear that it is "by grace" through faith that we are saved. "Grace is the source, faith the condition, of salva-

---

9. Such as when he referred to "original sin" instead of repentance in one of his summaries of the grand doctrines of the Methodists. See note 2 above.

tion" (#1, 118).[10] As with all of his mature thought, grace is everywhere, although it is by no means irresistible.

But more specifically, what manner of faith is under discussion here? First of all, it is not the "faith of a heathen." Such a faith entailed believing in "the being and attributes of God, a future state of reward and punishment, and the obligatory nature of moral virtue" (#1, 119).

Secondly, Christian faith is not "the faith of a devil." This faith of a devil assents to what the heathen believes, but in addition the devil knows that "Jesus is the Son of God, the Christ and the Saviour of the World" (#1, 119). Christian faith is neither (thirdly) that which the apostles had while Christ was on earth, for the power of his death and resurrection was not yet available. So what is the Christian faith?

> It may be answered: first, in general, it is faith in Christ—Christ, and God through Christ, are the proper object of it. Herein therefore it is fully distinguished by this—it is not barely a speculative, rational thing, a cold, lifeless assent, a train of ideas in the head; but also a disposition of the heart. For thus saith the Scripture, "With the heart man believeth unto righteousness." And, "If thou shalt confess with thy mouth the Lord Jesus, and shalt believe with thy *heart* that God hath raised him from the dead, thou shalt be saved." (#1, 120; emphasis his)

In further explaining this, he says that such faith saves us from guilt and fear, though "Not indeed from a filial fear of offending, but from all servile fear . . ." (#1, 122). Likewise, such faith gives peace and leads to rejoicing "in hope of the glory of God. . . . 'And the love of God is shed abroad in their hearts through the Holy Ghost which is given unto them'" (#1, 123; citing Rom 5:5). Finally, those who truly believe will use all of the ordinances, do good works, and "enjoy and manifest all holy and heavenly tempers, even the same 'mind that was in Christ Jesus'" (#1, 125; citing Phil 2:5).

This same structure of alternately describing what a Christian is *not*, then saying what a Christian *is*, can also be found in sermon number 2, "The Almost Christian." The almost Christian has honesty, truth, justice, and love as well, though only a love "that would not prejudice oneself."

---

10. Unless otherwise indicated, all references to Wesley's sermons are to the *Bicentennial Edition of the Works of John Wesley.* The sermon number followed by the page will be given in parentheses after the quote.

Such people even have "A form of godliness" though it is only "the *out-side* of a real Christian" (#2, 131–32; emphasis his). But beyond this, the almost Christian can even have "sincerity," a "real, inward principle of religion from whence these outward actions flow" (#2, 134).

But what, then, is implied in being "altogether a Christian?" Nothing other than the love of God, the love of our neighbor, the faith that purifies the heart and yields repentance and good works. He sums this up at the close of the sermon by saying:

> May we all thus experience what it is to be not almost only, but altogether Christians! Being justified freely by his grace, through the redemption that is in Jesus, knowing we have peace with God through Jesus Christ, rejoicing in hope of the glory of God, and having the love of God shed abroad in our hearts by the Holy Ghost given unto us! (#2,141)[11]

Denying that faith-as-assent is *by itself* enough to make one a Christian is found throughout the sermons and this can be seen as the obverse of his emphasis on the affections. Compare sermon number 4, "Scriptural Christianity": "'Christianity'; not as it implies a set of opinions, a system of doctrines, but as it refers to men's hearts and lives" (# 4, 161); and number 7, "The Way to the Kingdom": "He may assent to all the three creeds . . . and yet 'tis possible he may have no religion at all, . . ." (#7, 220); and number 62, "The End of Christ's Coming": "and least of all dream that orthodoxy, right opinion, (vulgarly called *faith)* is religion. Of all religious dreams, this is the vainest; which takes hay and stubble for gold tried in the fire! . . . Take no less for his religion, than the 'faith that worketh by love;' all inward and outward holiness" (#62, 483; citing Gal 5:6); and, finally, number 130, "On Living Without God":

> I believe the merciful God regards the lives and tempers of men more than their ideas. I believe he respects the goodness of the heart, rather than the clearness of the head; and that if the heart of a man be filled (by the grace of God, and the power of his Spirit) with the humble, gentle, patient love of God and man, God will not cast him into everlasting fire, prepared for the devil and his angels, because his ideas are not clear, or because his conceptions are

---

11. For some mature modifications to his rather unqualified categories in "The Almost Christian," see his 1787 sermon "The More Excellent Way," sermon number 89.

confused. "Without holiness," I own, "no man shall see the Lord;"
but I dare not add, "or clear ideas." (#130, 175)

Related to this is Wesley's assertion that we should let reason do all
that it is capable of and not undervalue it, but neither should we over-
value it. For we must acknowledge that reason is "utterly incapable of
giving either faith, or hope or love; and, consequently, of producing either
real virtue, or substantial happiness. Expect these from a higher source,
even from the Father of the spirits of all flesh" (#70, 600).

As seen in this last passage, Wesley's stress on happiness and holiness
as the marks of the Christian life is present in these published sermons, as
it was throughout his writings. Indeed, Outler mentions in a note in his
introduction to the sermons that the correlation of happiness and holiness appears in no fewer than thirty of Wesley's sermons.[12] It is even used
negatively in number 78, "Spiritual Idolatry," where we are told that the
best way to keep ourselves from idols is to "be deeply convinced that none
of them bring happiness" (#78, 111).

The couplet "happiness and holiness," as well as the individual component words, appears in Wesley's *Notes Upon the New Testament* almost
as often as the word "love." While the term "happiness" can conjure images of a kind of insipid shallowness, Wesley was using the term in the
classical way that Plato and Aristotle used it. Wesley was a *eudaemonist*—
that is, he held that the true end of the human being was happiness—and
true happiness meant happiness in God, which implied "holiness," thus
the constant conjunction of these terms. He even translates "makarioi"
as "happy" in the Beatitudes instead of "blessed" (as the *Philips* and *Good
News* translations also do). The "children of light" therefore are "The
children of God; wise, holy, happy" (John 12:36).[13] Likewise "So great a

12. *Works*, 1:35 n. 28.

13. When referring to Wesley formal reflections on scripture, I will be quoting from
his *Explanatory Notes Upon the New Testament* (henceforth, *N.T. Notes*), which was first
published in 1756; and his *Explanatory Notes Upon the Old Testament* (henceforth, *O.T.
Notes*) initially published in installments over three years, 1765–1767. The reprint of this
latter work to which I will refer was published by Schmul Publishers of Salem, Ohio, in
1975. While one should keep in mind that the *O.T. Notes* do not have the same ecclesi-
astically normative status as the *N.T. Notes*, they can still be a good source of Wesley's
views, especially when seen through the editorial analysis done by Robert Casto in his
"Exegetical Method in John Wesley's *Explanatory Notes Upon the Old Testament*." Casto
sorted out Wesley's own comments from those interpreters he borrowed from, specifi-

salvation—A deliverance from so great wickedness and misery, into so great happiness and holiness" (Heb 2:3); and "Is for the present grievous, yet it yieldeth the peaceable fruit of righteousness—Holiness and happiness" (Heb 12:11) Thus, even the end of humanity is cast in terms of that which satisfies the heart most fully, that affective enjoyment of completeness: happiness.[14]

Wesley reproduced the same Preface in every edition of his sermons that appeared in his lifetime from 1746 to 1787. In it he wrote ". . . I now write (as I generally speak) *ad populum*—to the bulk of mankind—to those who neither relish nor understand the art of speaking, but who notwithstanding are competent judges of those truths which are necessary to present and future happiness."[15] At the conclusion of his thirteen-part series of sermons on the Sermon on the Mount, Wesley summarizes this pivotal collection of sermons—as well as his whole eudaemonistic vision of Christianity by saying, "In a word, let thy religion be a religion of the heart" (#33, 698).

This last reference to his series of sermons on Jesus's Sermon on the Mount calls for expansion, because seeing what Wesley thought was key in Jesus's central discourse shows the heart to be central. How this series of thirteen sermons has been edited recently also shows recent scholarship's apparent downplaying of this central aspect of Wesley's thought.

---

cally Matthew Henry and Matthew Poole. Thanks to Casto's work, it is only Wesley's own original comments to which I will refer in this present work. Regarding the *N.T. Notes*, given their normative status, I will not try to get "behind" the text through redaction criticism. For good or ill, Wesley recommended this work to his Methodists, so I will take a canonical approach to this. When referring to either work, I will assume that the Scripture references are themselves enough documentation to find the quotes, so I will not provide more detailed footnotes. When a passage contains a dash (—) the material quoted before the dash is the Scripture passage itself (KJV, sometimes slightly amended by Wesley), while what follows the dash is Wesley's comment. In addition to the dashes, Wesley and his subsequent publishers have used italics to differentiate Scripture from his notes. When reproduced in quotes, this pattern of dashes and italics can disrupt the flow of the passage so much that it can be harder than necessary to discern Wesley's points. Accordingly, while I have typically tried to preserve the dashes (—) when they occur to separate comment from Bible, I have avoided the use of italics except as needed to provide emphasis. Aside from these editorial adjustments, all of the words will be reproduced as they are in the original text of the *Notes*.

14. Just a few of the references to happiness and holiness in Wesley's *N.T. Notes* include: 1 John (Introduction), Matt 6:10, Matt 5:3, Matt 5:12, Matt 5:48, and 1 Cor 15:31.

15. *Works*, 1:103–4.

In sermon number one in the series, Wesley says that this divine discourse is divided into three principal branches, with the fifth, sixth, and seventh chapters of Matthew each dealing with one of the branches. These he describes as:

> In the first the sum of all true religion is laid down in eight particulars, which are explained and guarded against the false glosses of man in the following parts of the fifth chapter. In the second are rules for that right intention which we are to preserve in all our outward actions, unmixed with worldly desires, or anxious cares for even the necessaries of life. In the third are cautions against the main hindrances of religion, closed with an application of the whole. (# 21, 474–75)

What is most important for our concern here is that Wesley describes the "beatitudes" as "the sum of all true religion . . . in eight particulars." Wesley then, in sermons 1, 2, and 3 in the series, goes on to describe each of the beatitudes in terms of the affections of the heart. Poverty of spirit, mourning, being meek, hungering, and thirsting after righteousness, being merciful, pure in heart, being peacemakers, and being persecuted for righteousness sake are powerfully described in these sermons in terms of what it is like from the "inside perspective," so-to-speak, for the Christian to try to embody these eight aspects of true religion.

Yet, surprisingly, the most commonly used contemporary anthology of Wesley's sermons omits these three sermons from his series on the Sermon on the Mount.[16] Instead, his Sermon on the Mount series begins in this anthology with number four, on social religion. Whatever the motivation for this redaction, the absence of these sermons reinforces the appearance of scholarly diffidence about how heart-centered Wesley's theology truly was, and itself shows the need for a deeper understanding of Wesley's views of heart religion to be more widespread.

Perhaps most telling of what Wesley thought was central to Christianity is his "Plain Account of Genuine Christianity" (which started out as a letter to Conyers Middleton), Wesley begins his account not by asking the typically person-*independent* question of "What is *Christianity*?" but instead opens by asking the very person-dependent— and *affection-dependent*—question: "*Who* is a *Christian*?" His answer tells

---

16. See Outler and Heitzenrater, *John Wesley's Sermons.*

us that a Christian is marked by *humility*, that the "ruling temper of his heart" is absolute submission to God and the tenderest *gratitude*, that the Christian is above all marked by *love*, which is productive of *all right affections*, and he has no *fear of dispraise*, for since God *loves him*, human dispraise is not to be feared.[17]

He begins this account of "genuine Christianity," then, by first writing about what the personal enfleshment of Christianity looks like, and he expresses this in terms of the affections or tempers of the heart. Only *after* this is done does he turn to discussing what Christianity itself is. But even at that point, it is crucial to note the very *person- and affection-dependent* way in which he describes "Christianity."

He asks "what is real, genuine Christianity—whether we speak of it as a principle in the soul or as a scheme or system of doctrine?" Seemingly reinforcing his opening reflections on the "true Christian," Wesley here says that Christianity is capable of being seen as a "principle in the soul." But what about Christianity as a "scheme or system of doctrine?" Well, this scheme's primary accomplishment is to "describe the character above recited"—that is, theology's first job is to describe what Christianity looks like when it is enfleshed by describing the affections it engenders.

What comes next for theology? It should "promise this character shall be mine (provided I will not rest till I attain)" and then it should tell us "how I may attain it." He concludes this passage by saying

> May every real Christian say, 'I now am assured that these things are so; I experienced them in my own breast. What Christianity (considered as a doctrine) promised, is accomplished in my soul.' And Christianity, considered as an inward principle, is the completion of all those promises. It is holiness and happiness, the image of God impressed on a created spirit, a fountain of peace and love springing up into everlasting life.[18]

Wesley then immediately begins section III of this piece by saying "And this [inward principle or holiness] I conceive to be the strongest evidence of the truth of Christianity. I do not undervalue traditional evidence. . . . And yet I cannot set it on a level with this."[19]

17. "A Plain Account of Genuine Christianity," first published in 1753, now found in Outler, *John Wesley*, 183ff.

18. Ibid., 191.

19. Ibid.

This last statement may sound dangerously close to making irrelevant the historical bases of our faith, giving the appearance, for instance, that the twenty-first-century arguments between the "Jesus seminar" and people like N. T. Wright are irrelevant. These historical arguments are *not* irrelevant for Christianity today, and Wesley would not have seen them as irrelevant in his time, as witnessed by his many arguments with the deists of his day. But Wesley's statement that this "inward principle" is the "strongest evidence of the truth of Christianity" helps us see just how central the renewed human heart is to his entire theological vision.

Another sermon that speaks to Wesley's emphasis on the person-relative understanding of Christianity is number 4, "Scriptural Christianity." In describing Christianity, his threefold analysis discusses "Christianity" as it begins to exist in individuals (speaking about repentance, faith, and love), then as it spreads from one individual to another, and then, finally, as it covers the earth. He closes with a blast against the Oxford of his day, asking where are these people who are supposed to be filled with the Holy Ghost, love of God and love of neighbor?

The evidence already displayed makes it clear that, for Wesley, true religion consists, in great part, of having religious affections. To round out our considerations, I will share just a few other pieces of evidence from his work that show his consistent emphasis on a *person-dependent* description of Christianity, a vision that he frames in terms of the affections of the heart:

- In his sermon "The Law Established by Faith, Discourse II" he saw "faith"—understood as both the summary of the cognitive content of the creeds and Scripture *and* as an experience of trust—as only the *handmaid* to love (#36, 38). The faith on which some Protestants lay virtually their whole emphasis is, in other words, merely the door into the larger house of love and all of the "fruit of the Spirit" that lie within it for Wesley.

- In his sermon "Of the Church" he described "the walk worthy of the vocation wherewith we are called" in terms of the attitudes of the heart such as lowliness, humility, meekness, long suffering, forbearing one another in love, living in peace (#74, 53).

- In his sermon "Justification by Faith" Wesley speculated that God made faith to be the necessary *means* to receiving justification because having to step out in faith, and not having absolute certainty, is an action that works against pride (#5, 597–98). He sees God's concern for human heart formation, then, to be reflected even in the means (faith) that God has selected for the God-human relationship.

- In the Preface to his *Christian Library* he quotes 1 John 4:19 saying that the Christian religion is "nothing stranger, or harder to understand than this, 'We love Him, because He first loved us.'"[20] Compare this with the addition to his Preface to his *Sermons on Several Occasions* that he inserted in 1788:

  > I think a preacher or a writer of Sermons has lost his way when he imitates any of the French orators. . . . Only let his language be plain, proper and clear, and it is enough. God himself has told us how to speak, both as to the matter and the manner: "If any man speak," in the name of God, "let him speak as the oracles of God;" and if he would imitate any part of these above the rest, let it be the First Epistle of St. John. This is the style, the most excellent style, for every gospel preacher. And let him aim at no more ornament than he finds in that sentence, which is the sum of the whole gospel, "We love Him, because He first loved us."[21]

  When we look at his comment on this passage in the *N.T. Notes*, we see that this scripture is at the center of Wesley's theology:

  > We love him, because he first loved us—this is the sum of all religion, the genuine model of Christianity. None can say more: why should any one say less, or less intelligibly? (1 John 4:19)

- In the opening section of *An Earnest Appeal to Men of Reason and Religion* Wesley shows that love is the beginning of Christian doctrine and also the primary way of conceiving of God.[22] He also tersely describes the goal of his ministry by saying "You ask me what I would do with them. I would make them virtuous and

20. Found in the Jackson edition of Wesley's *Works*, 14:222.
21. *Works*, 2:357.
22. *Works*, 11:45.

happy, easy in them-selves, and useful to others" (51). He then goes on to emphasize that happiness is the proper concern of religion ("are you *now* happy?" 6off.) and that "inward" religion, the religion of the tempers, is what he preaches (63, 88ff.). In *A Farther Appeal*, Part I, he states that while we *are* meant to *feel* peace, joy and love, the best proof of being led by the Spirit is not merely a sensation but a "thorough change and renovation of mind and heart, and the leading a new and holy life."[23]

Given this unmistakable emphasis on the affections of the heart in his overall vision of Christianity, I want now to expand on Wesley's understanding of the human "heart" and how this relates to human reason. I will start by looking at Wesley's commentaries on Scripture, for, of course, Scripture is itself home to much heart language. This will set the stage for understanding the orienting concern of all of Wesley's theology—the renewal of the heart.

23. *Works*, 11:140–41.

2   Wesley and Scripture on the Heart and its Renewal

The Heart: The Venue for Happiness, Holiness, and True Christianity

As has been made clear by Robert Casto, Wesley borrowed heavily from other authors when he compiled his *Explanatory Notes Upon the Old Testament*.[1] Wesley intervened with his own comments in his editorially blended *O.T. Notes* most frequently when he thought a passage—in either the text itself or the comment by his sources Henry or Poole—could be interpreted in a Calvinist way. Specifically, whenever he saw indications of unconditional election, limited atonement, irresistible grace, or the necessary perseverance of the saints he took up his pen and set out to battle. Of special interest to us is the fact that many of these controverted passages deal specifically with the nature of the heart.

The issue first arises in Exodus where, on several occasions, Pharaoh's heart is "hardened." Commenting on 4:21 (where God says to Moses "I will harden his heart") Wesley states, "After he has frequently harden'd it himself, willfully shutting his eyes against the light, I will at last permit Satan to harden it effectually." Later, commenting on 7:13 ("and he hardened Pharaoh's heart") Wesley says, "That is, permitted it to be hardened." In 8:15 ("But when Pharaoh saw that there was a respite, he hardened his heart") Wesley points out that "he did it himself, not God, any otherwise than by not hindering." In 8:19 ("But Pharaoh's heart was hardened") Wesley adds, "By himself and the devil."

The same theme arises in Deuteronomy 2:30 where the text reads, "hardened his spirit" and Wesley adds, "That is, suffered it to be hardened." Likewise in Ps 105:25 ("He turned their heart to hate his people")

1. See note 13, chapter 1.

17

Wesley says, "That is suffered [allowed] them to be turned." Wesley makes the same kind of qualifying remarks twice in his comment on Ezekiel, once in his comment on Joel and again on Zechariah.[2]

The importance of these passages is twofold. First of all, we need to note that it is on passages concerning the heart, the spirit, the "inner" arena, that Wesley chooses to make his stand against Calvinistic double-predestination. Showing that God is never the source of evil through his comments on language about the heart, Wesley is saying that language concerning the heart can, and does, touch on issues fundamental to the faith.

Secondly, by making the editorial comments that he did, Wesley is saying that even the heart, that often mysterious entity of the human being, is, at least to some extent and on some occasions, understandable and, in fact, in our control. The hearts of the Biblical figures never were hardened or turned, according to Wesley, without at least the complicity of the person himself. Humanity's freedom extends into the very inner life of the heart.

So far, then, we can say two things about the heart on Wesley's view. First, the heart is crucial for Christianity. It is not only, or even primarily, the source of irrelevant impulses or merely irrational passions that need to be tamed. The heart is the arena of the individual person where Christian truth is either exhibited or found wanting.

Secondly, the heart is fundamentally our own construction. Now, of course, nothing is ever *totally* our own construction for Wesley, if that is understood to imply "independent of grace." God's prevenient grace, according to Wesley, goes before us in everything we do. Charles Rogers in his "The Concept of Prevenient Grace in the Theology of John Wesley" shows this beyond doubt. But in our freedom, we can determine, and therefore are responsible for, the frame, the contents, the intentions, of our heart. While our own wildly different individual histories—including the sum total of all past inclinations, however acquired—provide a wide variety of starting places for spiritual growth, the final shape or form of our heart is to a great extent the result of own evaluations, judgments and decisions about how we choose to cooperate with God's grace.

2. Ezek 3:20 and 18:31; Joel 2:32, Zech 2:7. For more on his attacks on predestination, see his comments on Josh 24:16.

A corollary to this is that we can never totally suspend our judgment and rely only on intuitive impulses from our heart. There is no built-in guarantee that the heart will be right. This position, implied in Wesley's statements, finds the strongest possible support in the Old Testament literature.

Throughout the Old Testament text itself, independent of Wesley's comments, we find that when the Lord looks in judgment upon a human, it is not the outward appearance that is considered but the heart (e.g., 1 Sam 16:7, 1 Chron 28:9, Ps 7:9, Jer 11:20, 17:10, 20:12). This implies that the heart is not beyond the reach of human moral agency in some unfathomable darkness, but is in fact the *center* of moral agency. That a right heart is not some innate quality or some necessarily present "depth dimension" but, in fact, must be grown and developed, is seen clearly in the prayer of 1 Kgs 3:9: "Give therefore thy servant an understanding heart, to judge thy people, that I may discern between good and bad. . . ."[3]

Both the tendency of the unregenerate heart toward evil, and the possibility for it to change for the good are seen in Jeremiah. In 17:9 we find, "The heart is deceitful above all things and desperately wicked: who can know it?" But in 31:33 we read, "But this shall be the covenant that I will make with the house of Israel, After those days, saith the Lord, I will put my Law on their inward parts, and write it in their hearts, and will be their God, and they shall be my people." Similar passages can be found throughout the Scriptures, for example Ezek 36:26, which reads "A new heart also will I give you, and a new spirit will I put within you: and I will take away the stony heart out of your flesh, and I will give you a heart of flesh."

In Judg 21:25 we can see the insufficiency of the solitary human heart, the need for correction from outside of ourselves: "In those days there was no king in Israel; every man did that which was right in his own eyes." On this passage, Wesley comments, "What wonder was it then, if all the wickedness overflowed the land?" This shows that for Wesley, endless rummaging in our psyches is no guarantee of knowing the truth about God and what He has done for us. Introspection will only help us to know what we have already formed our hearts to be. The heart does not

---

3. Here and below I will be using the KJV of Wesley's *O.T. Notes.*

inherently hold all truth (as Socrates would have it), it holds only what we allow into it.[4]

This means that self-deception is always a possibility for Wesley, and this is a theme we see in his writings again and again. It is because the heart is quite fallible (not to mention the fact that we can, and often do, go against the leadings of our heart) that the act of repentance is so important, both liturgically and personally, for Wesley. This fact of human nature also necessitates the character trait of humility, which is a quality we will see Wesley recommend on many occasions.

To summarize Wesley's *O.T. Notes* on the heart, then, we can say that the heart is of central importance for Christianity, but to say this is not to exalt some necessarily and universally present internal set of norms and criteria for behavior. The heart can be many things, some good, some bad, but its ultimate nature and direction are directly affected by the human agent: for evil if guided only by the human, for good if God is sought as its ruler.

To assert this of Wesley does not mean that he is an irrelevant eighteenth-century curiosity who held that the blood-pumping muscle we know as the heart held mystical sway over the human being. Wesley used "heart" in the same metaphorical way that we do, to signify that part of the human that is most central, most important, the seat of values, the home of the deep and abiding emotions. Regarding the use of this term, we are no more primitive or advanced than Wesley. We still need to refer to our metaphorical center with some such term.[5]

That the heart is the locus for God's action in the human is also found throughout Wesley's *N.T. Notes*. On Rom 8:27 Wesley comments that it is the heart "Wherein the Spirit dwells and intercedes." On Col 3:2–3 ("Set your affections on the things above, not the things on the earth. For ye are dead and your life is hid with Christ in God") he comments, "For ye are dead—To the things on earth. And your real, spiritual life is hid from the

---

4. Today we would want to sound a note of caution here, aware as we are that the unconscious can have a powerful hold on us. Our history can betray our best intentions. But psychotherapy shows us that if we can consciously appropriate our history, it can cease to have a determinative influence on us. Thus, even the most secular therapist would, I think, ultimately agree with Wesley on human agency in the realm of human affectivity.

5. See Saliers, *Soul in Paraphrase*.

world, and laid up in God, with Christ Who hath merited, promised, pre-pared it for us, and gives us the earnest and foretaste of it in our hearts."

Echoing an Old Testament theme, Wesley says on Eph 5:19, "Singing with your hearts—As well as your voice. To the Lord—Jesus, who sear-cheth the heart." Similar to this is his comment on 2 Cor 3:3: "Written not in tables of stone—Like the ten commandments. But in the tender, living tables of their hearts God having taken away the hearts of stone, and given them hearts of flesh." On verse 6 of this same chapter he says, ". . . of the Spirit—Of the gospel dispensation, which is written on the tables of our hearts by the Spirit."

Luke 1:13 evoked this comment: "Thy prayer is heard—Let us ob-serve with pleasure that the prayers of pious worshipers come up with acceptance before God; to whom no costly perfume is so sweet as the fragrancy of an upright heart." Similarly, on Acts 15:9 he says, "Purifying . . . Their hearts—The heart is the proper seat of purity." Again, on Luke 3:8, "Say not within yourselves, We have Abraham to our father—That is, trust not in your being members of the visible church, or in any external privileges whatsoever; for God now requires a change of heart; and that without delay."

As in the *O.T. Notes,* though, there is no romanticism in his *N.T. Notes* about the heart having necessary and unmediated access to the truths of the universe. The heart is not stable and indelible but can change over time: "I have found David, a man after my own heart—This expres-sion is to be taken in a limited sense. David was such at that time, but not at all times. . . . We must beware of this, unless we would recommend adultery and murder as things after God's own heart" (Acts 13:22). And yet, without the heart, there is no true Christianity: "Their heart is far from me—And, without this, all outward worship is mere mockery of God." Again, in Mark 12:33:

> To love him with all the heart—To love and serve Him with all
> the united powers of the soul in their utmost vigor. And to love
> his neighbor as himself—To maintain the same equitable and
> charitable temper and behaviour toward all men, as we in like cir-
> cumstances, would wish for from them toward ourselves, is a more
> necessary and important duty than the offering the most costly
> and noble sacrifices.

The connection implied so far, namely, that between the heart and the affections, can be found in many places. One specific example should suffice for my purposes. Colossians 2:13 in the *N.T. Notes* reads, "the uncircumcision of your flesh—A beautiful expression for original sin, the inbred corruption of your nature, your uncircumcised heart and affections." This linking of the heart and the affections leads to the larger question of the logical connections that are implied by Wesley between the heart and the other faculties/capacities/functions of the "inner" life.

The heart is closely linked with the understanding or the mind for Wesley. On Eph 4:23 he says "The spirit of your mind—The very ground of your heart." The connection is even clearer in his comments on Luke 24:45, which reads: "But still they understood them [the Scriptures] not till He took off the veil from their hearts by the illumination of His Spirit." Again on Luke 24:25, "And slow of heart—Unready to believe what the prophets have so largely spoken," and Rev 2:23, "Shall know that I search the reins—The desires. And hearts— Thoughts."

And yet this intimate connection does not imply a total identification of all subjective functions and capacities, as seen in his note on Matt 6:31: "Every verse speaks at once to the understanding and to the heart." Even more explicit is his note on Rom 10:10 "For with the heart—Not the understanding only. Man believeth to righteousness. . . ." Similarly, to guard against an unwarranted reduction of heart language into mind language, we need to see that in some cases, the heart has to be right before the mind can function correctly:[6]

> Unsanctified learning made his bonds strong, and furnished him
> with numerous arguments against the gospel. Yet when the grace
> of God had changed his heart, and turned his accomplishments
> into another channel, he was the fitter instrument to serve God's
> wise and merciful purposes, in the defence and propagation of
> Christianity. (Acts 22:3)

The conscience is something else that is linked with the heart for Wesley, though "conscience" is a less important term for him in the *N.T. Notes*. Francis Glasson points out that Wesley dropped the only reference to conscience in the text of the Gospels when he deleted it from

---

6. Related to this, see contemporary philosopher William Wainwright's *Reason and the Heart* for a recent exposition of the view that reason functions best when informed by a properly disposed heart.

John 8:9.[7] Though Wesley used the term occasionally in his *Notes* (e.g., Luke 20:20 "Just men—Men of a tender conscience") he did not hold the natural human conscience in high regard, and in fact saw it as a highly fallible, humanly-formed faculty of judgment, which usually acts only to conform us to society. His note to 2 Cor 1:12 reads "The testimony of our conscience—Whatever others think of us."

The unreliability of the conscience can be seen in both Matthew's and Mark's depiction of Herod's role in the death of John the Baptist. On Matt 14:9 Wesley says, "And the King was sorry—Knowing that John was a good man. Yet for oath's sake—So he murdered an innocent man from mere tenderness of conscience!" Likewise, on Mark 6:26, "Yet for his oath's sake, and for the sake of his guests—Herod's honor was like the conscience of the chief priests. [Wesley here references Matt 23:6] To shed innocent blood wounded neither one nor the other."

The most complete statement about the heart and the conscience is found in his comment on 1 John 3:19:

> And assure our hearts before him—Shall enjoy the assurance of his favour, and the 'testimony of a good conscience toward God.' The heart, in St. John's language, is the conscience. The word conscience is not found in his writings.
>
> [verse] 20. For if *we have not this testimony, if in anything* our heart, *our own conscience,* condemn us, *much more does* God, *who is greater than our heart* [Wesley's interpolations in the Scripture text italicized]—An infinitely holier and a more impartial Judge. And knoweth all things—So that there is no hope of hiding it from Him.
>
> [verse] 21. If our heart condemn us not—If our conscience, duly enlightened by the word and Spirit of God, and comparing all our thoughts, words, and works with that word, pronounce that they agree therewith. Then have we confidence toward God—Not only our consciousness of His favour continues and increases, but we have a full persuasion, that 'whatsoever we ask we shall receive of him.'

There are two things worthy of note in this passage, the first relating to Wesley's subtle understanding of the biblical text. Wesley was sensitive to the variety among the many books of Scripture when he noted that

---

7. Glasson, "Wesley's New Testament Reconsidered."

the author of this epistle did not use the word "conscience" but in fact used "heart" to express the reality that Wesley referred to by the term "conscience." Wesley saw the flexibility of these terms and yet was able to convey a consistent meaning with them.

The second point to be drawn from this passage is that the conscience can be trusted only if it is enlightened by the Word and Spirit of God. Again, we find no infallible internal "depth dimension" universally present in natural humanity that can be consulted for ultimate truth. The person who is shut in on him- or herself has no reliable ally in his spiritual quest in the conscience.

Like "understanding" and "conscience," Wesley often links "spirit" and "soul" with the heart. For instance, in Rom 2:29 he states, "And the acceptable circumcision is that of the heart—Referring to Deut 30:6; the putting away all inward impurity. This is seated in the spirit, the inmost soul, renewed by the Spirit of God." His most explicit attempt to make clear the closely linked, though separate, meaning of these terms comes in his comment on Luke 10:27:

> Thou shalt love the Lord thy God—That is, thou shalt unite all the faculties of the soul to render Him the most intelligent and sincere, the most affectionate and resolute, service. We may safely rest in this general sense of these important words, if we are not able to fix the particular meaning of every single word. If we desire to do this, perhaps the heart, which is a general expression, may be explained by the three following. With all thy soul, with the warmest affection; with all thy strength, the most vigorous efforts of thy will; and with all thy mind, or understanding; in the most wise and reasonable manner thou canst, thy understanding guiding thy will and affections.

The Heart's Relations with Reason— and Reason's Contrary

Often in popular conception, emotions are considered to be not only "inner," but also "irrational," and, of course, in some circumstances, they might be (e.g., a debilitating fear of monsters under the bed). But when Wesley spoke about the religious affections, he had no such conception of irrational surds in mind. Here we must suppress our twenty-first-century culture's "common sense" notions about "emotion" if we are to understand Wesley's position.

Regarding the rationality of Wesley's thought in general, it is true that Wesley had some scornful things to say about natural, unaided human reason. His note on Acts 17:18, for example, reads:

> What would this babbler say?—Such is the language of natural reason, full of, and satisfied with, itself. Yet even here St. Paul had some fruit; though nowhere less than at Athens. And no wonder, since this city was a seminary of philosophers, who have ever been the pest of true religion.

Elsewhere he speaks of the "pride" of reason (Acts 17:32) and the instability of reason (Acts 28:6). But this did not mean that he had no use for reason, far from it. The true Christian has reason beyond the ken of the natural man, as seen in 1 Cor 14:20: "But in understanding be ye grown men—Knowing religion was not designed to destroy any of our natural faculties, but to exalt and improve them, our reason in particular."

This reason that has been "exalted" by religion is very far from being opposed to the religious affections. So far are the religious affections from being "irrational" on Wesley's terms that there is, in fact, a necessary connection between the religious affections and "reason" (or "understanding," "judgment," or the "knowing" faculty—all these terms are used in a roughly equivalent manner in the *Notes,* though they can be differentiated in other circumstances.)

This necessary connection can be seen, first of all, in the many passages where the "mind" is said to contain both the understanding and the affections. The note to Col 1:21 reads, "In your mind—Both your understanding and your affections" and that on 1 Pet 1:13 reads, "Gird up the loins of your mind— . . . so gather ye up all your thoughts and affections." Similarly, the note on Jas 1:5 refers to the "affections of the mind" and that on 1 Cor 2:3, commenting on the phrase "in fear and trembling," reads, "The emotion of my mind affecting my very body."[8]

---

8. This issue of the connections between the heart and the mind is one example where looking at the original Greek of the text can be of benefit. Where Rom 12:16 reads "agree in the same affection toward each other" and Col 3:2 says "Set your affections on the things above," the Greek in both cases uses a word that could be translated as "Mind ye" (*phronountes; phroneite*).

That there is "reason," or some engagement of the mind, in the affections for Wesley is seen in his many reminders that knowledge is to direct our tempers or "zeal." On Gal 4:17–18 he says, "Their zeal is not according to knowledge. . . . True zeal is only fervent love." Commenting on Rom 10:2, he diagnoses the malaise of his age: "They have zeal, but not according to knowledge—They had zeal without knowledge; we have knowledge without zeal." This same theme can be seen in his comment on 1 Cor 14:6, where he says, "Doctrine—To regulate your tempers and lives."[9]

On Titus 2:4 Wesley speaks about how wives are to love their families: "With a tender, temperate, holy, wise affection." This obviously implies the tempering of the affections by the faculty of judgment. This is also found in Matt 6:9: "Hallowed be thy name—Mayest Thou, a Father, be truly known by all intelligent beings, and with affections suitable to that knowledge!"

The mirror image of this can also be seen when Wesley talks about "inordinate affection" in 1 Thess 4:6, or "immoderate sorrow" in John 16:12. But the role of reason or judgment in the "inner" life of the believer is nowhere clearer than in Wesley's note to 1 Cor 14:32:

> For the spirits of the prophets are subject to the prophets—But what enthusiast considers this? The impulses of the Holy Spirit, even in men really inspired, so suit themselves to their rational faculties, as not to divest them of the government of themselves, like the heathen priests under their diabolical possessions. Evil spirits threw their prophets into such ungovernable ecstasies, as forced them to speak and act like madmen. But the Spirit of God left His prophets the clear use of their judgment, when, and how long it was fit for them to speak, and never hurried them into any improprieties either as to the manner, or time of their speaking.

Note here also the implied rejection of a solely supernatural or disruptive understanding of the Holy Spirit. Grace completing nature is a common Wesleyan theme.

Wesley is again on solid biblical ground in his emphasis on the constant role of judgment or reason in the Christian life. Passages such as

---

9. This understanding of doctrine invites a comparison with George Lindbeck's "regulative" understanding of doctrine, as spelled out in chapter 4 of his *Nature of Doctrine*, as well as with the general theme of Ellen T. Charry's *By the Renewing of Your Minds*.

1 John 4:1 ("try the spirits whether they are of God") and 1 Thess 5:21 ("prove all things, hold fast that which is good") show that the authors of Scripture never intended Christianity to be an exercise in uncritical intuition.[10] The constant presence of the judging faculty also helps to prevent any easy slide into self-deceptive affective/religious practices.

The above analysis of Wesley's emphasis on the affections and the heart makes a strong case for seeing that the renewing of the heart was the most essential element of Wesley's vision of Christianity. Indeed, from the very "Preface" to his *Sermons*, we see Wesley's emphasis on the life of the heart. In that Preface, Wesley says that in compiling these sermons it was his desire:

> First, to guard those who are just setting their faces toward heaven
> . . . from formality, from mere outside religion, which has almost
> driven heart-religion out of the world; and secondly, to warn those
> who know the religion of the heart, the faith which worketh by
> love, lest at any time they make void the law through faith, and so
> fall back into the snare of the devil. [11]

In his Sermon on "Original Sin" Wesley says, "Ye know that the great end of religion is to renew our hearts in the image of God" (#44, 185). Albert Outler comments on this passage that this renewal of the heart is the "axial theme of Wesley's soteriology,"[12] and almost every thinker who has studied Wesley agrees that soteriology is at the center of his theology. In light of this, and all of the other evidence here marshaled, I think it is safe to say that the orienting concern of Wesley's whole theological vision, the concept that shaped his whole theological enterprise, is best conceived of as *the renewal of the human heart*.[13]

---

10. Contrast this to F. D. E. Schleiermacher's *The Christian Faith*, section 3, where he states that true piety is neither a knowing or a doing but a feeling, an immediate self-consciousness. This work first appeared in 1821–22 and is available in English translation.

11. *Works*, 1:106

12. *Works*, 2:185n.

13. Two recent thinkers, who have no reason to sound Wesleyan, have described religion in a similar fashion to Wesley's vision of the renewal of the heart. John Cottingham, in his *Spiritual Dimension* says, ". . . the idea of a moral gap between how we humans are and what we aspire to be, is central to the religious impulse" (74). Similarly, C. S. Lewis, in his *Mere Christianity* says that the change from *bios* to *zoe* is "what Christianity is about" (159).

The Renewal of the Heart as Wesley's Orienting Concern

In his influential study of Wesley's theology, Randy Maddox terms Wesley's "orienting concern" to be "responsible grace."[14] With reference to Gerhard Sauter's use of an "orienting concept,"[15] Maddox sees an "orienting concern" as what gives consistency to, and provides guidance for, the various particular theological activities that a thinker undertakes. He sees an orienting concern to be "an abiding interest which influences the selection, interpretation, relative emphasis, and interweaving of theological affirmations and practices."[16] However, I would suggest that "responsible grace" does not do justice to Wesley's vision the way that "the renewal of the human heart" does.

I assert this not to deny that "responsible grace" can be a helpful heuristic device for understanding many of Wesley's theological concerns, especially his theological anthropology and the issue of God's providence. I do not see my proposal as *denying* Maddox's, but as offering an alternative that can live in harmony with his, as Maddox himself allows that a thinker might have more than one orienting concern.[17] I offer this alternative for several reasons.

First, the term "responsible grace" seems to domesticate and tame God's most lavish and extravagant gift to humanity. God's grace, seen especially in the forgiveness of sinners, is, from a human standpoint, the most irresponsible and incomprehensibly loving act that has ever occurred—something that no responsible *human* would ever do—and that is why such almost incomprehensible grace is supposed to engender comprehensive and life-changing gratitude, humility and love in the recipient.

To speak of Wesley's orienting concern as "responsible grace" also gives a second-order theological abstraction precedence over the first order realities of heart renewal to which Wesley devoted his life. True, Maddox's way of characterizing Wesley's vision may seem to give Wesley's thought more possibility of acceptance in the modern guild of theologians. This is true especially where Barth reigns, whose followers often see

14. Maddox, *Responsible Grace*, 17ff.

15. Ibid., 258 n. 16.

16. Ibid., 18.

17. Ibid., 18.

Schleiermacher crouching behind any reference to the life of the "heart" and hurriedly pull up the drawbridge of dialogue when they hear anything smacking of emotion. But, as I hope to make clear, these associations between Wesley's use of "the heart" and nineteenth-century romanticism are simply wrong, and when Wesley's emphasis on the renewal of the heart is undervalued, his entire theological vision is violated.

Related to this, as Maddox sees it, an "orienting concern" is typically "implicit,"[18] and this stipulation serves Maddox well since, as he notes, Wesley himself never explicitly used the phrase "responsible grace."[19] Maddox sees an "orienting concern" as "meta-conceptual" and not just one concept or metaphor among others. However, I do think there are real advantages to seeing Wesley's orienting concern as expressed in a conceptuality that Wesley actually used and spoke about.

I agree with Maddox's assessment that Wesley is concerned to "preserve the vital tension between two truths that he viewed as co-definitive of Christianity: without God's grace, we cannot be saved; while without our (grace-empowered, but uncoerced) participation, God's grace will not save."[20] However, when Wesley actually addressed such issues, he typically used the language of the heart, and moving away from this first-order language of love fear, hope and joy to a conceptuality as abstract as "responsible grace" distorts both the substance and the style of Wesley's theology.

Some readers might express a variety of concerns about taking the "renewal of the heart" as Wesley's orienting concern. They might point out that Wesley talked about heart *and life,* was concerned with *social* holiness, emphasized the life of the church, especially its sacraments, and that Wesley emphasized the life of the mind and education.

However, understanding in a detailed way what Wesley meant by "heart religion" and the "affections" will alleviate all of these concerns. To that task we will turn in chapter four. But first I want to step back from the eighteenth century and jump back into the twenty-first. I do this because over the last several years the Western intelligentsia have started to analyze and understand affective phenomena in ways that allow us to

18. Ibid., 258 n. 19. See also Maddox's "The Recovery of Theology as a Practical Discipline," 671.

19. Maddox, *Responsible Grace*, 259 n. 21.

20. Ibid., 19.

appreciate in a new way what Wesley was after with his program of heart religion.

So, having firmly established that Wesley's vision of Christianity was all about the renewal of the human "heart" and its "affections," we will now see how these realities are best understood today. We can then bring this current theoretical understanding of affective reality to bear on Wesley's views. This can then help us decide if Wesley's "heart religion" is best left as an embarrassing footnote in the history of the church, or if, instead, it is a paradigm with integrity that can produce praiseworthy fruits today.

PART II

*Wesley's "Heart Religion" Meets
Twenty-First-Century Emotion Theory*

3

Overcoming the Obstacles to Hearing Wesley's Voice Today

"Affections" Then, "Emotions" Now—
What's the Difference?

As has been clearly established, Wesley's theology would not be Wesley's theology without the language of the heart. What I want to look at now are the specific words and concepts that Wesley used to describe the "heart" realities of true Christianity. What was Wesley's vocabulary of the heart, and is it possible to map that vocabulary onto our current vocabulary? I hope to show that our understanding of "emotion" is not the same as what Wesley meant by the heart's "affections," and if we are to understand his vision, we must self-consciously filter and translate our own frames and guiding conceptualizations of affective reality.

We have seen that "heart" is used by Wesley as Scripture used it, and as we often use it today—as a metaphor for the essential core of a human being—the "home" of values, desires, hopes. But we have also seen his use of terms like "affections" that sound foreign and even quaint to our ears. The "foreignness" of these words, though, is something that is indicative of crucial conceptual differences between Wesley's age and ours. These key issues surrounding the vocabulary of the heart are pointedly raised in Thomas Dixon's book *From Passions to Emotions: The Creation of a Secular Psychological Category*.[1] Dixon rightly sees that the biggest problem in comprehending what people like Wesley were saying is understanding how our modern concept of "emotion" has blinded us to what Wesley saw as essential to "affections."

---

1. Dixon, *From Passions*.

The Shift in Vocabulary and Concepts between the Eighteenth and Twenty-first Centuries

In his book, Dixon, a Fellow of the Royal Historical Society and lecturer in History at the University of London, shows that the "emotions" came into being as a distinct psychological category in the nineteenth century replacing such terms as appetites, passions, sentiments, and affections. The domination of this category of "emotion," Dixon shows, has not been helpful. In fact, the over-inclusivity of this term has blinded us to the tremendous range of mental states that people actually experience. On Dixon's analysis, it is clear that the typical modern psychological understanding of emotion can distort what we might think Wesley meant by the affections.

Starting his historical survey with a study of passions and affections in Augustine and Aquinas, Dixon shows that Aquinas's "affect" was equivalent to Augustine's "affections" and that both were voluntary movements of the will, active and ascribable both to the angels and to God as well as humans.[2] Both these thinkers criticized the Stoics, who understood all affectivity as a kind of mistake, as not being able to distinguish between the virtuous affections and vicious "passions."[3] For these thinkers, the proper *object* of the affection makes all the difference. Dixon quotes Augustine's *City of God*:

> If these emotions (*motus*) and affections (*affectus*) which spring from a love of what is good and from holy charity are to be called vices, then all I can say is that real vices should be called virtues. However, the fact is that when such affections (*affectiones*) are directed to their proper objects, they follow right reasons, and no one should dare to describe them as diseases (*morbos*) or vicious passions (*passiones*).[4]

The voluntary nature of the affections was underscored by Aquinas in his *Summa*: "Man does not move immediately because of aggressiveness or desire, he waits for the command of the higher appetite, the will . . .

---

2. Ibid., 46.

3. For a contrasting evaluation of the Stoics understanding of emotion, one that sees the Stoics celebrating at least a small class of emotions, see Margaret R. Graver's *Stoicism and Emotion*.

4. *City of God* XIV.9, quoted in Dixon, *From Passions*, 47.

So a lower appetite is not enough for a human motion unless the higher appetite agrees."[5] Dixon notes the importance of this statement since the will "was implicated in any action, even if it was the result of a passion. . . . Hence while it might suffer passions it was responsible for making the decision to follow or to frustrate those passions."[6] Affections, then, are actions of the rational soul, while passions were actions of the irrational soul.[7]

In short, these medieval theologians introduced a critical distinction between sinful movements of the soul which would target the wrong objects and grow passions, versus the virtuous and potentially godly movements that

> were enlightened acts of the higher will—affections. Thus they made some psychological, moral and theological distinctions that were made neither in the classical discourse of the passions (*pathe*) nor in the subsequent discourse of the 'emotions.' This was the result of the Christian desire to say both—against the Stoics—that some human feeling or affection is proper and necessary to this life, but also that God, the angels and perfected humans are free from the turmoil and perturbations of sin and the passions. This was the heart of Christian affective psychology.[8]

Dixon, in his historical overview, jumps from Aquinas to the Age of Reason, and we see here that people like Jonathan Edwards and John Wesley are still using the terminology of the affections as Aquinas and Augustine used them. (Interestingly, Dixon never uses one of Wesley's favorite terms for affective reality—"temper"—and it is not to be found in his otherwise extensive index.) We see, however, that the roots for a change in conceptuality are starting to be sent out.

According to Dixon, the famous Scot David Hume laid the conceptual groundwork for this change in the eighteenth century when he wrote of

---

5. *ST* Ia.81.3, quoted in Dixon, *From Passions*, 53.

6. Dixon, *From Passions*, 53

7. Ibid., 58.

8. Ibid., 61. A more nuanced assessment of the Stoics can be found in Graver's *Stocism and Emotion*. Graver makes the case that, for the Stoics, some emotions were always irrational, such as anger and fear, but that joy and love were not.

passions (rather than persons) 'choosing means' to achieve desired ends. In fact will, along with reason, was reduced by Hume to one felt impulse among many others. . . . So the two pillars of a classically conceived Christian soul—will and reason—vanished in Humean psychology, to be replaced by a multitude of passions, sentiments, affections, desires or emotions, each the product of the learned associations of certain impressions with other impressions of pleasure or pain in past experience.[9]

Dixon claims that it is this secular and "scientific" sense of "emotions" as independent impulses or forces that has been the typical meaning for that English term ever since.

Later German thinkers, such as Immanuel Kant in his *Critique of Judgment* and his *Anthropology,* and Arthur Schopenhauer in his *The World as Will and Representation,* take a slightly different tack to the question of human nature, but to the same effect of throwing out the classical view of rational affections. These thinkers describe a tripartite model of the soul, where in addition to understanding and will a third faculty of feeling (*Gefühl* or *Empfindung*) was added. Now the groundwork was laid for theories that could picture passions and emotions as both irrational and involuntary. They could be "seen as alien powers rather than movements integral to the self."[10]

This came to explicit fruition later in the nineteenth century in the work of the Scot Thomas Brown, whom Dixon dubs "the inventor of the emotions."[11] (Dixon claims that the cumulative work of Hume, Brown, and Thomas Chalmers led to "The Scottish creation of 'the emotions'—the title of Dixon's fourth chapter.) In his vastly influential *Lectures on the Philosophy of the Human Mind,* Brown propounded that the first subdivision that needs to be made in his subject matter is between "our intellectual states of mind and our emotions."[12] Ever after this, finding the intellectual component in affectivity—something assumed in the classical view of "affections"—will be impossible, as emotions and the intellect have been ruled separate by definition.

9. Dixon, *From Passions,* 106.

10. Ibid., 97.

11. Ibid., 109.

12. Quoted in ibid., 98.

The upshot of this is traced by Dixon through the rest of the nineteenth century, through William James into the dominant contemporary psychological view, which he characterizes as being in the Hobbesian-Humean non-realist tradition. Dixon says that there were two important elements to this way of conceptualizing the will:

> First, the non-realist taught that 'will' was a word used to describe not a power or faculty, but a feeling. Secondly, the non-realist taught that, just as there was no faculty or power of 'will', so there were no other autonomous faculties, and certainly no autonomous self, 'having' sensory impressions, feelings and ideas. All that really existed for the non-realist was the stream of impressions, feelings and ideas themselves. For Brown these were characterized as 'sensations', 'emotions' and 'thoughts.' For James they became the 'stream of consciousness.'[13]

The difference in terminology, then, between "emotion" talk and "affections and passions" talk was more than a mere verbal difference, more than an updating of quaint language. The realities that these words seek to identify are quite different from one another. As Dixon puts it, the verbal difference led to "a difference in doctrine."[14] "Emotions" from the nineteenth century onward came to be associated with positivist and reductionist theories, where they are seen as involuntary—"mini-agents in their own right, rather than movements or actions of a will or self . . . non-cognitive states . . . to be contrasted with intellectual judgments and thoughts . . . aggregates reducible to physical feelings: they were 'worked up' from bodily sensations."[15] At its most extreme, this view sees all "emotions" as epiphenomena, pseudo-realities that have no significance in themselves.

This means that if we are to understand what Wesley meant by "heart religion" we must bracket what our modern world has invited us to believe about "emotions" and try to see them as Wesley did, through the conceptualities that gave rise to the terminology of "affections." Fortunately, we have powerful allies in this task, namely many contemporary philosophers and theologians who have recognized the conceptual bankruptcy of the Brownian, physicalist view of emotion and have labored in helpful ways to

13. Ibid., 250.
14. Ibid., 250.
15. Ibid., 251.

re-envision what "emotions" truly are. Of most interest for our concerns in this study is the fact that their re-visioning of the "emotions" leads to a view very consistent with what Wesley meant by the "affections."[16]

Contemporary Theoretical Inquiry into the Nature of Emotion

The number of philosophical studies of emotion published in the last few years has mushroomed to such an extent that even a listing of bibliographic resources could fill an entire volume in itself.[17] My purpose here is not to try to compile such an exhaustive list, but to give a sense of a few of the important common themes and arguments that mark this recent body of reflection. My focus will be on several thinkers who emphasize what might be broadly characterized as cognitive theories of emotion.

In looking at the work of contemporary thinkers Martha Nussbaum, Robert C. Roberts, and Paul Lauritzen, I will be able to show how several contemporary thinkers from different perspectives have come to evaluate emotion in common ways, and, further, have applied their analyses to morality and religion. After establishing a few theoretical points about the nature of emotion by looking at their work in this chapter, I will then be able to, in the following chapter, take a more detailed look at Wesley's vision of Christianity to see if his views are consistent with these contem-

16. I should note here at the end of this section on the conceptual change that has taken place in the last 200 years that Randy Maddox has given his version of the change specifically in Methodist theology from the time of Wesley through the nineteenth century. See his "Change of Affections." Maddox focuses on the influence of Thomas Reid and his "decisionistic rational control" model of moral psychology as one of the prime reasons Methodists strayed from Wesley's vision of heart religion (23–25). Interestingly, Dixon shows great familiarity with Reid's work, but he sees Reid as one of the defenders of the "cognitive affection" view that Dixon saw Wesley holding: "The cognitive view was used here by Reid in defence of Christianity and in opposition to Hume's anti-Christian reductionism" (Dixon, *From Passions*, 96). Maddox is probably right that the shift from Wesley's views to Reid's is a real one, but Dixon's larger point is also true—if everyone still believed as Reid, our views of "emotion" would be a lot closer to Wesley's "affections" than to reductionistic views—either those of Hume or their contemporary counterparts.

17. See, for example, the bibliographies in Martha Nussbaum's *Upheavals of Thought*, 715–34, and Solomon and Calhoun, *Thinking about Feeling*, 279–92. See also the lists of references in Neu, *A Tear is an Intellectual Thing*, 315–30, and Griffiths, *What Emotions Really Are*, 259–76.

porary views of affectivity. This will lead us to the final chapters where we will see how Wesley's vision of Christianity as "heart religion" could be seen though a new lens and perhaps provide a fresh model for theologizing and spiritual formation.

Martha Nussbaum's *Upheavals of Thought: The Intelligence of Emotions*

Martha Nussbaum is Ernst Freund Distinguished Service Professor at the University of Chicago with a joint appointment in the philosophy department, the law school, the divinity school, and the college. In 2001 her thick and detailed study of emotion *Upheavals of Thought: The Intelligence of Emotions* was published.[18] Her multi-disciplinary faculty position is reflected in the wide range of her book, which draws widely on philosophical and psychological reflection, as well as literary works and aesthetic theory. The title of the book comes from a quote from Marcel Proust's *Remembrance of Things Past* that I reproduce here:

> It is almost impossible to understand the extent to which this up-heaval agitated, and by that very fact had temporarily enriched, the mind of M. de Charlus. Love in this way produces real geological upheavals of thought. In the mind of M. de Charlus, which only several days before resembled a plane so flat that even from a good vantage point one could not discern an idea sticking up above the ground, a mountain range had abruptly thrust itself into view, hard as rock—but mountains sculpted as if an artist, instead of taking the marble away, had worked it on the spot, and where there twisted about one another, in giant and swollen groupings, Rage, Jealousy, Curiosity, Envy, Hate, Suffering, Pride, Astonishment, and Love. [19]

Nussbaum is taken by this description of emotions as "upheavals of thought," but she is at pains to avoid any idea that emotions should primarily be seen as impediments to clear thinking. It is not as if the flat plane of a barren landscape would be the desired goal from which emotions deter us. On the contrary, for Nussbaum, the emotions are "essential

18. Nussbaum, *Upheavals*.
19. Nussbaum, *Upheavals*, vii.

elements of intelligence."[20] Emotions are the medium through which we discern what it is we truly value. Parsing out the reason that emotions contain allows us to understand, as her subtitle indicates, the "intelligence of emotions."

Nussbaum says about emotion's role in philosophy and ethics what I think John Wesley would say about emotion's role in theology:

> emotions are suffused with intelligence and discernment, and if they contain in themselves an awareness of value or importance, they cannot, for example, easily be sidelined in accounts of ethical judgment as so often they have been in the history philosophy. Instead of viewing morality as a system of principles to be grasped by the detached intellect, and emotions as motivations that either support or subvert our choice to act according to principle, we will have to consider emotions as part and parcel of the system of ethical reasoning. We cannot plausibly omit them, once we acknowledge that emotions included in their content judgments that can be true or false, and good or bad guides to ethical choice.[21]

But to say this much about emotions is not to say that we must give emotions a privileged place of trust, or regard them as immune from rational criticism

> for they may be no more reliable than any other set of entrenched beliefs. There may even be special reasons for regarding them with suspicion, given their specific content and the nature of their history. It does mean, however, that we cannot ignore them, as so often moral philosophy has done.[22]

Nussbaum's book is divided into three main sections: "Need and Recognition"; "Compassion"; and "The Ascents of Love." It is the first section, where she lays out her theory of emotion that will be most pertinent to our interests. As the title of this first section implies, Nussbaum sees emotions as judgments that relate our own need for happiness (understood in the classical, "eudaemonistic" sense of the term) to the variety of objects that present themselves to us.

---

20. Ibid., 3.
21. Ibid., 1.
22. Ibid., 2.

As Nussbaum puts it, emotions are "intelligent responses to the perception of value."[23] As she sees them, emotions are "appraisals or value judgments which ascribe to things and persons outside the person's own control great importance for that persons own flourishing."[24] Her view thus

> contains three salient ideas: the idea of a *cognitive appraisal* or *evaluation*; the idea of *one's own flourishing* or *one's important goals and projects*; and the idea of the *salience of external objects as elements in one's own scheme of goals*. Emotions typically combine these ideas with information about events in the world; they are our ways of registering how things are with respect to the external (i.e., uncontrolled) items that we view as salient for our wellbeing.[25]

As Nussbaum makes clear, her theory has its antecedents in the ideas of the ancient Greek Stoics. This may surprise some familiar with the popular stereotype of "stoic" people as having no discernible affective life. But while Nussbaum endorses the Stoics' view that emotions involve evaluations, she rejects their normative view that the evaluations involved in emotions are typically false.

In fact, Nussbaum takes the reader through several stages of refinement on the Stoic view, including denying the Stoic position that animals have no emotions, making allowances for the social construction of emotions, and limning a developmental view of how adult emotions are closely related to formative experiences in infancy and childhood. For this latter view, she borrows much from current psychologists in the "object-relations" tradition (though she also draws deeply from the work of the great French novelist Marcel Proust whom she calls "in some ways the most profound object-relations psychoanalyst of all"[26]). Before her theoretical musings are through, Nussbaum's remarkable analysis also turns to music, which she sees as a source of "non-linguistic cognition."

I will make no pretense to covering all of these themes in depth as Nussbaum does over the course of seven hundred pages. I want to focus on her view that emotions are cognitive evaluations. It will perhaps best

23. Ibid., 1.
24. Ibid., 4.
25. Ibid.
26. Ibid., 7.

illustrate what she means by this if we clearly understand what Nussbaum sees as the "adversary" to her cognitive-evaluative view. This is the position that sees emotions as

> non-reasoning movements, or unthinking energies that simply push the person around, without being hooked up to the ways in which she perceives or thinks about the world. Like gusts of wind or the currents of the sea, they move, and move the person, but obtusely, without visions of an object or beliefs about it. In this sense they are 'pushes' rather than 'pulls.' Sometimes this view is connected with the idea that emotions derive from an 'animal' part of our nature, rather than from a specifically human part—usually by thinkers who do not have a high regard for animal intelligence.[27]

Nussbaum maintains that though this view of emotion is grossly inadequate, it has been very influential, especially in some scientific circles. (With Dixon's historical analysis, we can see how this "adversary" view came to be.)

As a way of making clear her own view of emotion, Nussbaum narrates her own grief over her mother's death. By paying close attention to this narrative, Nussbaum makes clear her own cognitive view of emotion while also showing the "adversary" theory to be bankrupt. Nussbaum sees at least four ways that the emotions stirred up by her mother's death are unlike the "thoughtless natural energies" of the adversary's view. First, they are *about* something: they have an object.

> My fear, my hope, my ultimate grief, all are about my mother and directed at her and her life. A wind may hit against something, a current in the blood may pound against something: but they are not in the same way *about* the things they strike in their way. My fear's very identity as fear depends on its having some such object: take that away and it becomes a mere trembling or heart-leaping. The identity of the wind as wind does not in the same way depend on any particular object against which it may pound.[28]

This leads to her second point, that the object is an *intentional* object, by which she means that this object figures in the emotion as it is seen or interpreted by the person whose emotion it is.

---

27. Ibid., 24–25.
28. Ibid., 27.

Emotions are not *about* their objects merely in the sense of being pointed at them and let go, the way an arrow is released toward its target. Their aboutness is more internal, and embodies a way of seeing. My fear perceived my mother both as tremendously important and as threatened; my grief saw her as valuable and as irrevocably cut off from me.[29]

Her third reason why emotions are more than unthinking bodily experiences is that emotions embody beliefs about the object—often very complex beliefs. Nussbaum quotes Aristotle (who, of course, is the same source that so informed Aquinas and his cognitive understanding of affectivity) to show that in order to have fear, one must believe that bad events are impending and that I am not entirely in control of warding them off. In order to have anger, I must have an even more complex set of beliefs: "that some damage has occurred to me or to something of someone close to me; that the damage is not trivial but significant; that it was done by someone; probably, that it was done willingly."[30] She goes on to point out that these beliefs are essential to the identity of the emotion: "the feeling of agitation all by itself will not reveal to me whether what I am feeling is fear or grief or pity. Only an inspection of the thoughts discriminates."[31]

Her final point on showing the inadequacy of the reductionistic "adversary" view concerns one particular aspect of the intentional perceptions and the beliefs characteristic of an emotion:

they are concerned with value, they see their object as invested with value or importance . . . [this value is] of a particular sort. It appears to make reference to the person's own flourishing. The object of the emotion is seen as *important for* some role it plays in the person's own life. . . . Another way of putting this point . . . is that emotions appear to be eudaimonistic, that is, concerned with the person's flourishing. . . . emotions look to the world from the subject's own viewpoint, mapping events onto the subject's own sense of personal importance or value.[32]

It is this framework for understanding emotions that allows Nussbaum to call hers a "cognitive" view. By cognitive Nussbaum means "nothing

29. Ibid.
30. Ibid., 29.
31. Ibid.
32. Ibid., 30–33.

more than 'concerned with receiving and processing information.' I do not mean to imply the presence of elaborate calculation, of computation, or even of reflexive self-awareness."[33]

If these aspects of affectivity are accepted at face value, and I think Nussbaum presents a compelling case, then the reductionistic, non-cognitive, Brownian view of the "adversary" theory must be rejected and the cognitivity of emotions must be acknowledged. Before moving on to some of the other pertinent thinkers that can help us frame an understanding of Wesley's heart religion, I want to consider one point raised by Nussbaum's analysis.

Part of Nussbaum's book is concerned with the course of development of particular emotions in the infant and child, including shame, love, and disgust. While this developmental emphasis is important for Nussbaum, I do not think her basic insights into the nature of emotion stand or fall with her developmental analysis. I think this becomes obvious when we understand a set of distinctions first made apparent to me in a systematic way by the philosopher G. D. Marshall in a little article called "On Being Affected," though Nussbaum does not refer to it. In this piece, Marshall distinguishes between the object of an emotion, the occasion of an emotion, and the cause of the emotion. Allow me to illustrate how these three differ one from another, and then I will come back and show the pertinence of this distinction for my sidestepping Nussbaum's developmental point.

I will take Marshall's own example of delight to illustrate the distinction: "The object of one's delight, for example, may be a certain piece of music, the occasion, a particular performance of the work, the cause, whatever it is that has made one like this sort of music at all."[34] One might think of a parallel example using this same analysis, say, the emotion of anger. We might say that a particular politician is the *object* of one's anger, seeing the politician speak on television is the *occasion* for experiencing the anger, and the *cause* of the anger is that politician's decisions, with which one disagrees.

I give Marshall's analysis, and the two examples to illustrate it, in order to show that one need not accept Nussbaum's psychoanalytic theory about the development ("cause") of any particular emotion in order to

33. Ibid., 23.
34. Marshall, "On Being Affected," 243.

accept her larger view of the cognitivity of emotion. That is why I have chosen not to outline her theory on that point in any depth. With regard to the cause of particular emotions, I think Marshall's relaxed sense about causation, reflected in his statement that "whatever it is that has" caused a particular emotion, is specific enough of a way to refer to the cause of particular emotions for most of our purposes. The relative truth of Freudian or object relations theory as regarding how any particular emotion is first caused, does not necessarily qualify our considerations of the object-relatedness of emotion or the cognitivity of emotion, and it is those points that will be most salient when we come back to consider Wesley's views.[35]

Robert C. Roberts's *Emotions: An Essay in Aid of Moral Psychology*

Martha Nussbaum is explicit in her book about her conversion from Christianity to Judaism. For her, Judaism gives the moral sphere more centrality and autonomy, and she considers the Christian doctrine of original sin as making it seem impossible for humans to become, and be, good.[36] She allows for possible exceptions for Thomistic conceptions of Christianity, and I would hasten to add that Wesleyan exceptions should be added to her qualified rejection of Christianity on moral grounds. Nonetheless, she writes from a consciously non-Christian view.

Robert C. Roberts, on the other hand, is Distinguished Professor of Ethics at Baylor University and, while a philosopher by profession, has written several works from an explicitly Christian point of view.[37] While his book, *Emotions: An Essay in Aid of Moral Psychology*,[38] is a philosophical approach taken with the goal of clarifying certain aspects of ethics, he obviously sees no contradiction between his understanding of ethical responsibility and his Christian faith. What is of most interest to me in

35. For a recent discussion of the cause of emotions in regard to developmental stages and Wesley's own context, see Haartman's *Watching and Praying*.

36. Nussbaum, *Upheavals*, 549–51.

37. See, for example, *Strengths of a Christian, Spirituality and Human Emotion*, and *Spiritual Emotions*.

38. Roberts, *Emotions*.

this book, though, is how Roberts and Nussbaum agree on many of the key questions concerning the nature of emotion.

Roberts lists twelve facts that any general "account" of emotion must take account of. Note here that Roberts prefers to speak of an "account" rather than a "theory." An *account*, for him, can be a series of discussions that test a certain paradigm, while a *theory* of emotion would be a special kind of account that "purports to specify the necessary and sufficient conditions for anything's membership in the class emotion."[39] An account, then, he sees as being better suited to the subject of emotion—a number of particular features of emotion can be viewed together to form a paradigm for the concept, without pretending to be the last word on the subject.

Just as I did not elaborate all of Nussbaum's ruminations on emotion, I will not do so for Roberts's twelve facts. But for our purposes, it is important to show that like Nussbaum, Roberts holds that emotions are not the same as feelings (see his points one and two[40]). Related to this, Roberts takes seriously the attacks from those who want to reduce psychology to biology and neuro-physiology, and he has an extended critique of one of the recent attempts in this genre, Paul Griffiths' *What Emotions Really Are: The Problem of Psychological Categories.*[41]

Also like Nussbaum, for Roberts, emotions typically take objects (see his points three and four[42]). Again paralleling Nussbaum, Roberts sees emotions as crucial for morality (hence his subtitle "An Essay in Aid of Moral Psychology"), and he makes this explicit in his point eight where he claims that many types of emotion are motivational "in the sense that they involve the desire to perform characteristic types of action. . . "[43] Finally, Roberts sees cognitivity as undeniably present in emotion, especially as seen in his summary definition of emotion as "concern-based construals."[44]

I should point out that Roberts has a quarrel with Nussbaum with regard to her seeing emotions as "judgments" because, among other rea-

---

39. Ibid., 64.
40. Ibid., 60–81.
41. Ibid., 14–36.
42. Ibid., 61–62.
43. Ibid., 63.
44. Ibid., 64ff.

sons, judgments must involve assent. Roberts points out that the subject of an emotion need not assent to the emotion's claim. He thinks it is better to think of emotions as a kind of appearance, impression, or "construal" that tend to generate judgments than to think of emotions themselves as judgments.[45] Without denying the importance of these distinctions for Roberts's own views, I think what is most crucial here is that these two major contemporary theorists of emotion insist that the cognitive dimension of human consciousness is alive and very much active in the experiences we call emotions.[46]

At this point allow me to shift gears a bit from these philosophers whose concern is to show the importance of emotion for ethics, to a contemporary writer who takes the affective dimension seriously for specifically theological purposes.

Paul Lauritzen's *Religious Belief and Emotional Transformation*

There are a number of writers on religion who have written recently about themes that touch on religious experience in one way of another, including philosophers of religion speaking about the relative veridicality of different types of religious experience, or commenting on the variety of religious experiences and reflecting on some of the implications of these experiences.[47] But aside from these philosophers of religion, a relative few, but a growing number, of scholars of religion are writing about emotions per se and their normative role in the life of the believer.

First to be mentioned should be my mentor, Don E. Saliers of Emory University who has written on these matters in many places, including

45. Ibid., 83–106.

46. For a fuller listing of contemporary philosophers who support a cognitive view of emotion with references to their work, see 22–23 n. 2 of Nussbaum's *Upheavals*.

47. See, for example, Pojman, *Philosophy of Religion*, especially Section II, "The Argument from Religious Experience"; and Proudfoot, *Religious Experience*. One of the most promising philosophical texts that addresses affectivity and religion is Wainwright's *Reason and the Heart*. In this text Wainwright makes the case on philosophical grounds that ". . . (under the right circumstances) passion, sentiment and affection may be necessary conditions of using our cognitive faculties correctly" (154). On this last theme, see also *Emotional Experience and Religious Understanding* by Wynn, as well as *Spiritual Dimension* by Cottingham.

The Soul in Paraphrase.[48] But in a way that bears directly on our present concerns, Paul Lauritzen of John Carroll University has brought the concern for theological normativity to the analysis of emotion in ways that can shed light on Wesley's attempts to do so two centuries ago.

In his 1992 book *Religious Belief and Emotional Transformation: A Light in the Heart*,[49] Paul Lauritzen sets out to establish that religious beliefs can, in fact, transform emotions. In order to do this, he had to fight many of the same conceptual battles that our two philosophers, Nussbaum and Roberts, had to fight.

Leaning on the work of philosophers Robert Solomon and (especially) Charles Taylor, Lauritzen criticizes the purely physicalist approach to emotion of the natural sciences, where emotions are reducible to sensations, because this approach seeks to eliminate the role that self-understanding plays in human life: ". . . to understand human life apart from subjective properties is just to understand it apart from self-understanding."[50] But for Lauritzen, the importance of self-understanding is central and non-negotiable for Christians.

Calling on Hauerwas's and MacIntyre's emphasis on the importance of narrative, Lauritzen points out that narratives shape character "because they provide categories of self-understanding. . . . before I can answer the question 'What am I to do?' I must answer the question 'Of what story am I a part?'"[51] When the Christian narrative provides us with the self-understanding, for instance, that we are sinful yet redeemed, our faith is informing our self-understanding in fundamental ways and our self-understanding, "in turn, gives form and substance to our emotions.[52]"

This inescapable cognitive dimension of emotion is brought out even more explicitly when Lauritzen speaks about the "intentional" character of emotions.

---

48. See also the work of Richard Steele, especially his *"Gracious Affections" and "True Virtue" According to Jonathan Edwards and John Wesley*, as well as that of Henry Knight III, especially his *Presence of God in the Christian Life*, and Brooks Holifield's *History of Pastoral Care in America*.

49. Lauritzen, *Religious Belief.*

50. Ibid., 36.

51. Ibid., 31

52. Ibid., 30.

> . . . emotions are almost always about something. We are rarely, if ever, simply proud, angry or afraid. Rather we are angry *at* someone, proud *of* something, afraid *of* something or someone. . . . And when we ask about the object of anger, we are asking about the beliefs or judgments that make anger an appropriate response in a particular situation.[53]

All of this leads Lauritzen to offer the following definition of emotion:

> What then is an emotion? I suggest that we define an emotion as an experiential complex, shaped by social norms, that consists of such diverse elements as pronounced physiological activity, expressive bodily responses, feelings, desires, beliefs and evaluative judgments. Further, I suggest that we treat the cognitive components of the complex, beliefs and judgments, i.e., those components that embody self-understanding, as the keystone holding these various elements in place, for two reasons: (1) belief and judgment not only accompany the bodily responses characteristic of emotions, but cause them; and (2) without appeal to evaluative judgment we have no way of distinguishing emotional states, one from another.[54]

While Lauritzen's formulation is not as guarded and qualified as, say, Roberts's (e.g., Lauritzen's suggesting that bodily responses are a part of all emotion where Roberts said that this relationship holds only in some cases), we see here many of the key features of emotion emerging that we saw in the formulations of both Nussbaum and Roberts, especially the key role that belief/evaluative judgment play in emotion.

Lauritzen sees the power of narrative to shape distinctive communities, and the power of communities to shape self-understandings, and self-understandings shape emotions. Following this logic, one could expect that distinctive communities can be expected to have distinctive emotions. This is precisely what Lauritzen goes on to show.

In his fourth chapter, "The Emotions of Anger and Resentment," Lauritzen, like Nussbaum and Roberts both, refers to imaginative literature for examples of how beliefs shape emotion (which makes sense, given his emphasis on narrative). He picks four "angry episodes" from Steinbeck's *The Grapes of Wrath* to show how Western social norms governing anger

53. Ibid., 55.
54. Ibid., 65.

and resentment can be evinced. The examples include incidents where the protagonists' anger was justified (e.g., when directed at injustice), as well as when it was not justified (e.g., when a person's truculence was misinterpreted as being directed at the protagonist). Tying these incidents together, Lauritzen summarizes by saying that in our culture, "The expression of anger is an accusation of wrongdoing."[55]

Confirmation of this generalization about anger is also seen by Lauritzen in several anthropological studies. Lauritzen consulted field work on how the Taita people of Kenya deal with anger, and he also summarized some work done on Canadian native people. One of his most interesting findings was the evidence that confirmed his view of anger as related to wrongdoing among these Canadian natives.

Anger is apparently rarely found in adults found among the Utku Eskimos. The anthropologist studying them who observed this also had a theory that fits Lauritzen's view. According to this anthropologist, the Utku rarely get angry because they live in a society where one of the controlling concepts is *ayuqnaq*, which translates as "fatalism, an attitude of resignation to the inevitable."[56] If everything is fated and whatever happens is inevitable, then how could someone truly see something as "wrongdoing?" The Utku's understanding of their world and themselves is definitively shaped by their beliefs—and their emotions, or lack of same—are the inescapable result.

Summary of Key Theoretical Insights

As these representative thinkers have shown, there is a remarkable convergence in recent theorizing about the nature of emotion. The idea that emotions are purely sensory experiences that happen outside of the input or control of cognitive capacities must surely be rejected. The cognitive dimension of emotion can be seen in their intentional, or what we might say their *transitive*, nature: they take objects. These objects are typically defined by certain beliefs, judgments or construals. Not only that, but these belief-related experiences we call "emotions" function as motivations to act in certain ways, in other words, they function as dispositions

55. Ibid., 86.
56. Ibid., 88.

to behave. Following Lauritzen's linking of specifically metaphysical beliefs with our own self-understandings which lead to specific emotions,
we could say—like Wesley—that if we truly believe that all humans are
created in the image of God and all are sinful but absolutely loved, we
should be motivated to love one another as God has loved us, and to love
our neighbor as ourselves.

We are now ready to take this contemporary analysis of affectivity
and see if we can apply it to make sense of Wesley's vision of Christianity
as being about the "renewal of the heart."[57]

---

57. A final note on terminology. Two recent interpreters of Wesley have asserted that
there is an important difference in the way that Wesley uses the terms "affections" and
"tempers." Ken Collins in his article "John Wesley's Topography of the Heart," says that
while "disposition" and "temper" are used interchangeably by Wesley throughout his
writings, it is "a mistake to identify tempers and affections" (165–67). Similarly, Maddox
(whom Collins quotes on this subject) sees the "affections" and the "tempers" as sepa-
rable (*Responsible Grace,* 69–70; and his article "Shaping the Virtuous Heart," 27–28). I
have done a close textual analysis of Wesley's works to show that, in fact, Wesley often
uses "affection" and "temper" in interchangeable ways (see my "Wesley's Language of
the Heart"). Wesley even occasionally uses the term "emotion," but when he does it is
primarily to indicate a general sense of arousal or interest, e.g. *Journal* for Tues. May 6,
1760: "I had much conversation (at Carrickfergus) with Monsieur Cavenac, the French
General, not on the circumstances, but the essence, of religion. He seemed to startle at
nothing; but said more than once, and with emotion, 'Why, this is my religion: There
is no true religion besides it!'" (*Works* 21:259); and, again from his *Journal,* for May 2,
1741: "A few of our brethren and sisters sitting by, then spoke what they experienced. He
told them, (with great emotion, his hand trembling much,) . . ." (*Works* 19:192). In one
instance he puts "emotion" in apposition to affection. In defining zeal he says of the term
"When it is figuratively applied to the mind it means any warm emotion or affection"
(Sermon 92, "On Zeal," *Works,* 3:311).

4

Why Depth of Emotion Is not the Same as Intensity of Feeling

Having now seen Wesley's vision of Christianity as a program for the renewal of the heart, and then showing that we cannot assume that what we mean by "emotion" is at all what Wesley was talking about when he spoke of the "affections," let us now move to a more in-depth analysis of Wesley's understanding of the heart and its affections. In this we will try to discern the grammar or logic of the heart as Wesley saw it and see if his views of the heart are in fact compatible with the sophisticated cognitive views of today.

Informed by exposure in the previous chapter to the conceptualities of our contemporary theorists, we will be looking at several key aspects of his views of affectivity. These are: 1) the role of feelings in Wesley's heart religion and how they affect his understanding of Christianity, especially as seen in how he characterizes the doctrines of assurance, sin and perfection; 2) how Wesley thinks emotions are generated—specifically, whether or not he sees them as object- and judgment-related; and 3) whether Wesley saw the affections as necessarily expressing themselves in the actions of the believer—i.e., acting as dispositions to behave. I will deal with the first set of issues in this chapter, and the remaining two in the following chapter.

Experiencing the Affections— The Role of "Feelings" in Heart Religion

Wesley has often been called an "experiential" theologian. Especially since the normative thrust of Methodism has in the past been mischaracterized as a "quadrilateral" of Scripture, reason, tradition, and experience, much has been made of this distinctively Methodist element of "experience."

While Wesley may be considered, in one way or another, an experiential thinker, the terms "experience" or "experiential"—or its eighteenth-century cognate "experimental"—do not often appear in his comments on Scripture.

Three of the few examples of this usage to be found in the *N. T. Notes* are found in Ephesians and 1 Corinthians. Ephesians 1:18 reads "That ye may know the hope of His calling—That ye may experimentally and delightfully know what are the blessings which God has called you to hope for by His word and His Spirit." Ephesians 4:13 conveys a similar thought: "Till we all—And every one of us. Come to the unity of the faith, and knowledge of the Son of God—To both an exact agreement in the Christian doctrine, and an experimental knowledge of Christ as the Son of God." On 1 Cor 1:24, Wesley notes that while others may see Christ crucified as a stumbling block or foolishness, those who are called will "experience, first, that He is the power, then, that He is the wisdom, of God."

The limitations of "experience" as a theological term are clear in these passages. The major drawback, and it would be a decisive one for a practical thinker like Wesley, is that the term is too general, it is empty of actual content. To hear that we might "experimentally know the blessings that we hope for," to have "an experimental knowledge of Christ," to experience that "Christ is the power and wisdom of God" leaves one feeling rather at loose ends. The questions "How?" and "In what way?" come immediately to mind after hearing these injunctions.

The more concrete language of the particular affections bypasses these questions. Love, joy, fear, etc., are direct and specific and can be sought after by directing one's attention to those aspects of reality which evoke them, specifically, in the Christian context, the story of what God has done for us in Christ. While Wesley used "experience" and "experimental" in rather general and generous ways, the best way to comprehend his appeals to "experience" is by tracing out his discussions concerning specific affections and the logical relations between these affections and their contexts.

"Experience" was part of the eighteenth-century thinker's vocabulary primarily because of people like Locke who held that experience is the source of all knowledge. While Wesley can be linked with this school of thought, the "cash value" (to use William James's expression) of his use of the term "experience" in the Christian arena would, for Wesley, typically be some particular affection.

"Pleasure" and "Comfort"

Some thinkers of the nineteenth century, especially poets and others of the Romantic period, thought of Christianity mainly in terms of its ability to produce certain interior consolations, pleasures or comfort. This was not the case for Wesley. Pleasure and comfort played only a limited, contextual role in his *N.T. Notes*. These immediate positive sensations did not provide the basis for any large-scale decisions about the theological adequacy of a thought, doctrine or action. They were in no way the end of Christianity for John Wesley. But neither was avoiding them the duty of the Christian, as if being a Christian were the same thing as being a Stoic. Let us consider a few representative selections.

"Redeeming the time" in Eph 5:16 for Wesley means ". . . buying every possible moment out of the hands of sin and Satan; out of the hands of sloth, ease, pleasure, worldly business. . . ." If this were to stand alone Wesley could be accused of being a rather severe sobersides, but later in the same chapter he says, "But be ye filled with the Spirit—In all His graces, who gives a more noble pleasure than wine can do." In the same vein, Wesley interprets the twentieth verse of Philemon ("Refresh my bowels in Christ") to mean, "Give me the most exquisite and Christian pleasure." His distinctions about pleasure become clearest in 2 Pet 1:6, where he writes, "Christian temperance implies the voluntary abstaining from all pleasure *which does not lead to God*" (emphasis mine).

A similar set of distinctions applies to the term "comfort." While 2 Cor 13:11 ("Be of good comfort") means for Wesley, "Be filled with divine consolation," he says, commenting on Luke 15:14, that trying to satisfy oneself on worldly comforts is a "vain, fruitless endeavor!" Comforts, like pleasure, are recommended only on the basis of whether or not they are "worldly" or "divine," whether or not they are base or lead to God. Colossians 4:11 is another example of looking only to God for the comfort that is worth attaining: "Who have been a comfort to me?—What, then, can we expect? That all our fellow workers should be a comfort to us?"

One final quote on this topic deserves reproducing. Here we can see the nature of true comfort and what it does and does not imply. In 2 Cor

1:3 we find the phrase "The Father of mercies, and God of all comfort," on which Wesley comments, "Mercies are the fountain of comfort: comfort is the outward expression of mercy. God shows mercy in the affliction itself. He gives comfort both in and after the affliction. Therefore is He termed, the God of all *comfort*. Blessed be this God!" The comfort of God, then, is not something that rescues us from all affliction, but it comes to us *in* our affliction. Such is no simple-minded escapist pleasure. It is more like a reminder of the cross, and it echoes James 1, which speaks of joy in the midst of tribulation.

"Feelings," "Impressions," and "Impulses"

One might expect the most elemental language of experience—feelings, impressions and impulses—to be rampant in the pages of a book authored by someone who is often dismissingly called a "pietist" or "enthusiast." Indeed, there is some textual evidence that Wesley was concerned to recommend that Christians needed to be filled with certain feelings. The starkest passage to this effect is found in his comment on the last verse of 2 Pet 3:18:

> But grow in grace—that is, in every Christian temper. . . . Frames (allowing the expression) are no other than heavenly tempers, 'the mind that was in Christ.' Feelings are the divine consolations of the Holy Ghost shed abroad in the heart of him that truly believes. And wherever faith is, and wherever Christ is, there are these blessed frames and feelings. If they are not in us, it is a sure sign that, though the wilderness became a pool, the pool is become a wilderness again.

Here it is boldly asserted that a certain feeling is a necessary evidence for the presence of faith. Note, however, that there is no claim for *constant* "blessed frames and feelings." Examining the other germane quotes from the *N.T. Notes* shows us that the center of gravity of Wesley's position is that being intensely aware or conscious of certain feelings is only an episodic feature of the Christian life, not a perpetual state. Let us consider some examples.

On Acts 17:27, Wesley writes:

> If haply—The way is open; God is ready to be found; but He will lay no force upon man. They might feel after him—This is in the midst between seeking and finding. Feeling, being the lowest and grossest of all our senses, is fitly applied to that low knowledge of God. Though he be not far from every one of us—We need not go far to seek or find Him. He is very near us; in us. It is only perverse reason which thinks He is afar off.

Wesley is using "feeling" here in a slightly different sense than it was used in the previous quote.[1] But it is important, nonetheless, to note that in this passage feeling is regarded as the *lowest* of the senses. From feeling we can get a sense of the presence of God in some way, a way that reason cannot provide, but such low-level intuitions are hardly saving knowledge.

Related to this, there are three places in the *N.T. Notes* where an inward "impulse" is mentioned: In Matt 4:1, "By the Spirit—Probably through a strong inward impulse"; Luke 2:27, "By the Spirit—By a particular revelation or impulse from Him"; and Acts 7:23, "It came into his heart—Probably by an impulse from God." In all three cases, I have reproduced the whole passage; there was no further elaboration on these "impulses."

On Acts 16:7, however, Wesley makes a fuller, more telling comment: ". . . but the Spirit suffered them not—Forbidding them as before. Sometimes a strong impression, for which we are not able to give any account, is not altogether to be despised." Here we see that these impressions or impulses are hardly the key to his epistemology, they are merely "not to be despised." His was not a theology of sheer intuition and instinct.

Further evidence for the guarded and limited role that "feeling" (as conscious sensation) plays for Wesley's theology is found in Acts 18:5 where he says "Paul was pressed in spirit—The more, probably, from what Silas and Timotheus related. Every Christian ought diligently to observe any such pressure in his own spirit, and, if it agree with Scripture, to follow it: if he does not, he will feel great heaviness." Here the immediate experience is not given any autonomy at all, but is to be followed only "if it agree with Scripture."

Related to this is the intense experience of crying. On Acts 20:37 Wesley writes:

1. For a discussion of the difficulties surrounding the variety of uses of the term "feeling," see Gilbert Ryle's article titled "Feelings," where he differentiates seven different meanings for the term "feel."

> They all wept—Of old, men, yea, the best and bravest of men, were easily melted into tears; a thousand instances of which might be produced from profane as well as sacred writers. But now, notwithstanding the effeminancy which almost universally prevails, we leave those tears to women and children.

Here is no ringing challenge to go out and weep, only a bit of gentle irony about the current attitudes toward crying. This kind of intensity of feeling is in no way suggested to be a continuous norm for Christians. [2]

Even more telling is Matt 4:1 where, immediately after being baptized by John, Jesus is tempted by the devil: "After this glorious evidence of His Father's love, He was completely armed for the combat. Thus, after the clearest light and the strongest consolation, let us expect the sharpest temptations." There is no sign here of a continuity of feeling, an unbroken flow of pleasant awareness. The warning in the last line in fact seems to be a direct statement to the effect that we are not to depend on feeling since it is bound to fluctuate.

The strongest and, I think, most definitive, statement on this whole matter comes in Wesley's comment on 1 Thess 2:17. The Scripture verse reads: "But we, brethren, being taken from you for a short time, in presence, not in heart, laboured with great desire the more abundantly to see your face." This seemingly unimportant passage occasioned the following remarks from Wesley:

> In this verse we have a remarkable instance, not so much of the transient affections of holy grief, desire, or joy, as of that abiding tenderness, that loving temper, which is so apparent in all St. Paul's writings towards those he styled his children in the faith. This is the more carefully to be observed, because the passions occasionally exercising themselves, and flowing like a torrent, in the apostle, are observable to every reader; whereas it requires a nicer attention to discern those calm, standing tempers, that fixed posture of his soul, from whence the others only flow out, and which more particularly distinguish his character.

Here Wesley straightforwardly states it is the "calm, standing tempers, that fixed posture of the soul" that is indicative of character, not the exhibition of, or the self-conscious awareness of, any particular felt reality.

2. For a contemporary theoretical analysis that shows the powerful connections between tears and who we are as people, see Neu, *A Tear is an Intellectual Thing*.

Though I resist the conclusion that Collins and Maddox drew from this passage that affections are always pictured by Wesley as "transient" and tempers are always seen as "fixed,"[3] I do think we can see here Wesley's favoring of the stable and enduring aspects of affectivity which our contemporary theorists might term "emotion" as opposed to the short-lived realities they might term "feelings." In light of this, and all of the above quotes, I think we can safely say that the conditional statement found in Wesley's comment on 2 Peter (that if faith is present, then one will have certain feelings) is not to be taken to apply to all believers at all times. If one is to be a Christian, then one will have the kind of temper or character or affectional make-up from which the particular Christian affections will "flow out," but this is quite different than saying that a Christian is to be forever filled with certain intense sensations.

The Holy Spirit and the Assurance of Faith

The sensitive inter-play between our spirit and the Holy Spirit in the affections of the believer which we discerned in the *Notes* is again seen in the sermons. My interpretation of the *Notes* on this topic, namely that the Spirit is active, yet not in an overpowering way, is confirmed by Outler's introduction to the sermons, where he says that on Wesley's terms, the believer is "indwelt and led by the Spirit within rather than being possessed by the Spirit as if by some irresistible force."[4] The implications of this for the religious affections are seen especially in three sermons: "The Witness of the Spirit I," "The Witness of the Spirit II," and "The Witness of Our Own Spirit."

The first two of these sermons (both on Rom 8:16) were written over twenty years apart, yet both have the same goal in mind, namely, to show the enthusiasts how they "have mistaken the voice of their own imagination for this 'witness of the Spirit' of God, and thence idly presumed they were the children of God while they were doing the works of the devil!" (#10, 269). As usual, Wesley declined to specify *how* this assurance is worked in us (276)—he offers no schematic of our spiritual plumbing. Nonetheless, he maintains that there are several important conceptual clarifications that can and should be made.

3. See references in note 57 above, chapter 3.
4. *Works*, 1:75.

The most important point Wesley makes in these sermons is that there *is* a direct witness of the Spirit, but it never appears *without* its fruits which are, of course, the religious affections of peace, joy, love, etc. (see Gal 5:22–23, which Wesley quotes or alludes to on pages 279, 283, 286, and 297). One determines if one has this assuring witness, therefore, not by waiting for some Damascus road experience (though Wesley would never deny that such do in fact occur), but by determining if one loves God:

> He that now loves God—that delights and rejoices in him with an humble joy, an holy delight, and an obedient love—is a child of God;
>
> But I thus love, delight, and rejoice in God;
>
> Therefore I am a child of God;
>
> then a Christian can in no wise doubt of his being a child of God.
> (#10, 276)

In the later sermon he makes the same point: "When our spirit is conscious of this—of love, joy, peace, long-suffering, gentleness, goodness—it easily infers from these premises that we are the children of God" (#11, 289). In countering an objection to this, he also shows that "experience" has a limited role to play in determining the core of the gospel:

> It is objected, first, 'Experience is not sufficient to prove a doctrine which is not founded on Scripture.' This is undoubtedly true, and it is an important truth. But it does not affect the present question, for it has been shown that this doctrine is founded on Scripture. Therefore experience is properly alleged to confirm it. (#11, 293)

As always, the Bible is the final authority. "Experience" cannot by itself "prove" something relating to the Faith which is unscriptural.

In summarizing this theme, Wesley draws two inferences. The first is "let none ever presume to rest in any supposed testimony of the Spirit which is separate from the fruit of it" (#11, 297). The second is "Let none rest in any supposed fruit of the Spirit without the witness" (298). As he had said earlier,

> . . . to secure us from all delusion, God gives us two witnesses that we are his children. And this they testify conjointly. Therefore, 'what God hath joined together, let not man put asunder.' (#11, 295)

The third sermon in this series, number 12, "The Witness of Our Own Spirit," takes 2 Cor 1:12 as its text: "This is our rejoicing, the testimony of our conscience, that in simplicity and godly sincerity, not with fleshly wisdom, but by the grace of God, we have had our conversation in the world." The sermon, then, is "to show what is the nature and ground of a Christian's joy. We know, in general, it is that happy peace, that calm satisfaction of spirit, which arises from such a testimony of his conscience as is here described by the Apostle" (#12, 300).

Here we are thrown back to the language of "conscience" that we also encountered in the *Notes,* and, as in the *Notes,* Wesley at first appears to be proposing some universal principle present in all: "we may understand by conscience a faculty or power, implanted by God in every soul that comes into the world, of perceiving what is right or wrong in his own heart or life, in his tempers, thoughts, words, and actions" (#12,302). But here, as in the *Notes,* he qualifies this by saying that the conscience is determined by the "rule" which controls it, and this "rule" is quite different for Christians than the "rule" of the world (302). (Compare also 310 where Wesley shows that Christian joy is not a natural joy.) Here again we can see his absolute rejection of a naturalistic and autonomous ethical sense as proposed by Shaftesbury and Hutcheson, while at the same time he asserts that the testimony of a good conscience *is* part of his vision of the Christian life. These same themes are elaborated in sermon 105, "On Conscience."

The witness of our own spirit, then, is not an experience available to anyone (e.g. like Schleiermacher's "feeling of absolute dependence"), but only to *Christians* who have been formed in the Christian "rule" of the gospel, found in Scripture (302–3). If we are thusly formed, "If therefore this eye of thy soul be single, all thy actions and conversation shall be 'full of light', of the light of heaven, of love and peace and joy in the Holy Ghost" (306–7). This testimony or assurance, then, is not some necessary religious *a priori* to be mystically intuited; it is the contingent result of our taking as the object of our affections God and what God has done for us:

> We are then simple of heart when the eye of our mind is singly
> fixed on God; when in all things we aim at God alone, as our God,
> our portion, our strength, our happiness, our exceeding great re-
> ward, our all in time and eternity. This is simplicity: when a steady
> view, a single intention of promoting his glory, of doing and suf-

fering his blessed will, runs through our whole soul, fills all our heart, and is the constant spring of all our thoughts, desires, and purposes. (#12, 307)[5]

One last point needs to be made concerning Wesley's normative pronouncements about the Spirit and our affections. In sermon number 3 "Awake Thou That Sleepest," written by Charles Wesley, there is a rather bold claim made for either a clear and full assurance or none at all. In Outler's note to this he points out that "both brothers rather quickly modified this all-or-nothing emphasis by allowing for degrees of assurance."[6] The mature position of John regarding the stages of growth in faith is best represented by his distinction between the "faith of a servant" (characterized primarily by *fear* of God) and the "faith of a son" (characterized primarily by *love* of God).[7]

Sin, the Believer, and Perfection

The doctrine of Christian perfection was one that "God peculiarly entrusted to the Methodists" according to Wesley's *Journal* entry of February

5. In light of this, I have to take exception to Outler's "Introductory Comment" to these three sermons. On page 267 he says, "It was clear enough that Wesley's theory of religious knowledge was frankly intuitionist, but this had been all too easily misconstrued as a one-sided subjectivism." In order to rescue him from such "subjectivism," Outler interprets these three sermons as betraying the following logic:

> The main point to the discourses on 'The Witness of the Spirit' had been the *objective* ground of Christian assurance, *viz.*, the direct 'witness of the Spirit' as revealing to and convincing the believer of God's pardoning, regenerating, adoptive grace. Here, in the sequel, [sermon 12] Wesley undertakes an analysis of the *subjective* side of this *experience* of grace. (#12, 299 [emphasis his])

My objection to this is his terming the witness of the Spirit as "objective." As God's grace is quite resistible on Wesley's terms, no witness will ever be "objective" in the sense of being independent or our evaluations of it. Therefore, I think it is more helpful to say that God is the *object* of the experience rather than saying that the direct witness is "objective." If Outler meant by his phraseology "not self-generated," and this is my suspicion, then we are in fundamental agreement, but I think my language is less susceptible to misinterpretation.

6. *Works*, 1:154 n. 179. Outler refers here to John's letter of March 28, 1768, to Dr. Rutherford, and sermons 89, 106, and 117. See also the mature Wesley moving away from an all-or-nothing approach by comparing #2, "The Almost Christian," with #89, "The More Excellent Way."

7. See *Works*, 1:250 #9, "The Spirit of Bondage and Adoption," and especially Outler's n. 4.

6, 1789. It was also a doctrine that caused much confusion and misunderstanding about the affections since it was "perfect love" which Wesley was preaching. If perfection were required, many wondered, would the Christian then have to be feeling only one thing, namely love, at all times?

First of all, we need to understand Wesley's understanding of perfection. The best summary of it is found in sermon 76 "On Perfection":

> This is the sum of perfection: It is all comprised in that one word, Love. The first branch of it is the love of God: And as he that loves God loves his brother also, it is inseparably connected with the second: 'Thou shalt love thy neighbor as thyself.' Thou shalt love every man as thy own soul, as Christ loved us. 'On these two commandments hang all the Law and the Prophets:' these contain the whole of Christian perfection. (#76, 74)

Later in this same sermon he says that another way to talk about this whole reality of perfection is in terms of acquiring the mind of Christ, which includes "the whole disposition of his mind, all his affections, all his tempers, both toward God and man. Now, it is certain that as there was no evil affection in him, so no good affection was wanting" (#76, 74).

Yet it was clear, to Wesley above all, that Christians did in fact sin. Indeed, sermon 13, "On Sin in Believers," was concerned solely with "inward sin: any sinful temper, passion, or affection . . . any disposition contrary to the mind which was in Christ" (#13, 320). It is this kind of sin that can *remain* even though Christ *reigns* (#13, 323), or, as he says later in this sermon, Christians have crucified the flesh with its affections and lusts (Gal 5:24) yet this flesh remains "and often struggles to break free from the cross" (#13, 329). As Outler points out in his introduction to both "On Sin in Believers" and "The Repentance of Believers," Wesley wrote these sermons in the 1760s but inserted them in the first volume of his *Sermons* after some decidedly un-Wesleyan formulations of the doctrine of perfection were starting to circulate, especially among the Moravians.

"Sinless perfection" was not Wesley's term of choice, though some of his writing had been interpreted in that direction.[8] What we have, then, is an affectional *telos* for the Christian life—perfect love—which is in no

---

8. See Outler's n. 66 on Sermon 40, "Christian Perfection," where he points out how Wesley sometimes spoke unguardedly about "perfection" (*Works*, 2:107).

way contradicted or vitiated by affectional sin even in the justified believer. This reflects a basic feature of Wesley's theology: that justification and sanctification are two closely related yet logically separate realities. "A man may be in God's favour though he *feel* sin; but not if he *yields* to it" (#13, 332; emphasis his). We still need the "Repentance of Believers" (sermon 14) because while we are born again at the moment of justification, we are not entirely changed, nor wholly transformed, "Far from it" (# 14, 351). Acknowledging the reality of sin, however, should not keep us from having an "uneasiness for the want of [entire sanctification]," we need to "hunger and thirst after it" (#14, 351).

Having perfect love as our goal, then, does not mean that we must always have some constancy of inner *feeling*, which any psychologist (or any sentient being, for that matter) would say is impossible. Wesley never maintains that total control over the inner realm is somehow the norm for Christianity. In fact, inner feelings are not the issue at stake here. Just as we saw in the *N.T. Notes*, *feelings* can come and go, but it is the more enduring aspects of the affectional make-up which speak to the question of whether or not someone is a Christian:

> A man may have *pride* in him, may think of himself in *some particulars* above what he ought to think (and so be *proud* in that particular) and yet not be a proud man in his *general* character. . . . Resentment of an affront is sin. It is anomia, disconformity to the law of love. This has existed in me a thousand times. Yet it did not, and does not, *reign*. . . . *Here,* therefore, as in ten thousand instances, there is *sin* without either *guilt* or *power* (#13, 330–31; emphasis his)[9]

But too one sided of an emphasis on the "inner" aspect of the affections also moved Wesley to comment, as in his journal entry of January 25, 1738, where he describes his acquaintance with the mystic writers

> whose noble descriptions of union with God and internal religion made everything else appear mean, flat and insipid. But in truth, they made good works appear so too, yea, and faith itself, and

---

9. For other discussions of how negative affections can exist in the justified, though not yet sanctified, believer, see sermons #41, "Wandering Thoughts"; #46, "The Wilderness State"; and #47, "Heaviness Through Manifold Temptations." See also Outler's notes in *Works*, volume 1, about how Wesley repudiated "sinless perfection" (328 n. 1; 333 n. 102; and 346 n. 81).

what not? These gave me an entire new view of religion, nothing like anything I had had before. But alas! It was nothing like that religion which Christ and his apostles lived and taught. I had a plenary dispensation from all the commands of God . . . . Thus were all the bands burst at once .... Only, my present sense is this, All the other enemies of Christianity are triflers; the mystics are the most dangerous of all its enemies.[10]

In his journal of November 1, 1739, he also condemns the idea of "being still" (doing no works),[11] and it is this issue which caused his ultimate break with the Moravians, as Wesley recorded in his *Journal* of December 31, 1739.[12]

Wesley's experiences during a meeting held in a room on Aldersgate Street on May 24, 1738, are well known, but they nonetheless are worthy of a few comments here. Showing the transitivity or intentionality of emotion, which will be discussed more fully in the following chapter, Wesley states that before his Aldersgate experience he had faith "But still I had not this faith on its right object: I meant only faith in God, not faith in or through Christ."[13] But at that society meeting:

About a quarter before nine, while he was describing the change which God works in the heart through faith in Christ, I felt my heart strangely warmed. I felt I did trust in Christ, Christ alone for salvation; and an assurance was given me that He had taken away my sins, even mine, and saved me from the law of sin and death. . . . But it was not long before the enemy suggested, 'This cannot be faith; for where is thy joy?' Then was I taught that peace and victory over sin are essential to faith in the Captain of our salvation; but that, as to the transports of joy that usually attend the beginning of it, especially in those who have mourned deeply, God sometimes giveth, sometimes withholdeth them, according to the counsels of His own will.[14]

Both the proclamation of the felt presence of salvation, as well as the acknowledgement of its felt absence, then, were part of Wesley's experi-

---

10. *Works*, 18:213.

11. *Works*, 19:113–14.

12. *Works*, 19:131–34.

13. *Works*, 18:247.

14. *Works*, 18:249–50.

ence and message from the beginning. That there was never a pretense of an unbroken continuity of felt joy, or even peace or love or faith, in his own life can be seen in several despairing journal entries. Seven months after his "conversion," (January 4, 1739) he stated that "I am not a Christian now."[15] Even more strongly, twenty-seven years later he claims in a letter to his brother Charles that "I do not love God. I never did. . . . Therefore I am only an honest heathen."[16]

Despite such passing phases of his spiritual life, however, he always claimed that the radical change of conversion (his own and that of others) was real and he often described it in terms of the affections. "I have seen (as far as a thing of this kind can be seen) very many persons changed in a moment from the spirit of fear, horror, despair, to the spirit of love, joy, and peace, and from sinful desire, till then reigning over them, to a pure desire of doing the will of God."[17] Thus, even though he knew there was no guarantee of constant feeling, he always asserted that to be a Christian meant having certain affectional capacities. Such an emphasis led others to say he was "beside himself'"[18] and to give naturalistic, debunking explanations of the dramatic conversions his ministry facilitated[19], but his linking of Christianity and the religious *affections*, if not religious *feelings*, never changed during his entire life.

To reinforce these quotations and analyses, one can also see his qualified appraisals of felt-affectivity in:

- His *A Plain Account of Christian Perfection* where he guards against a religion of feeling by admonishing his readers to try all things such as "dreams, voices, impressions, visions, or revelations" by the Scriptures in order to judge if they are from God.[20]

- His long "Answer to the Rev. Mr. Church" where Wesley states directly how Christians *must* speak about the "inner" life *without* uncritically proclaiming a religion of feeling. There he asks:

15. *Works*, 19:29.
16. *Letters*, Telford, ed., 5:16.
17. *Journal* May 20, 1739. *Works*, 19:59.
18. *Journal* May 7, 1739. *Works*, 19:55.
19. *Journal* May 21, 1739. *Works*, 19:60.
20. Jackson *Works*, 11:429.

Do you reject inward feelings *toto genere?* Then you reject both the love of God and of neighbor. For, if these cannot be inwardly felt, nothing can. You reject all joy in the Holy Ghost; for if we cannot be sensible of this, it is no joy at all. You reject the peace of God, which, if it be not felt in the inmost soul, is a dream, a notion, an empty name. You therefore reject the whole inward kingdom of God; that is, in effect, the whole gospel of Jesus Christ.[21]

- In his 1739 Preface to the book that most clearly links the aesthetic to the religious, his *Hymns and Sacred Poems,* he clearly warns against reducing religion into feeling states by pointing out that "The Gospel of Christ knows of no religion but social; no holiness but social holiness. 'Faith working by love' is the length and breadth and depth and height of Christian perfection."[22]

Summary on Feeling and the Affections for Wesley

Now we can return to the distinction between experiencing an emotion and the emotion itself. In the language of G. D. Marshall, as discussed in chapter 2, the *experience* of an emotion on a particular occasion can be distinguished from the emotion itself. It is this *experience of the emotion* that I think is most helpfully termed "feeling." Feeling here is clearly the more transitory or "ephemeral" reality, whereas an emotion entails the underlying judgment or construal that makes possible the occasional experience of feeling. Perhaps an example would help make this clear.

If a man loves his wife, this does not entail that he will be *feeling* that love at all waking moments. When he is balancing his checkbook or changing his oil or leading a meeting at work, chances are slim that he will be feeling intense, passionate love for his wife. Nevertheless, if we saw the big picture of his life and could note that he took his wife's concerns to be as important as his own, that he shared his time and money and energy with her, that he went out of his way to have positive relationships with

---

21. Jackson *Works,* 8:408.

22. Jackson *Works,* 14:321. See also *Works,* 7, Appendix I, 'Thoughts on the Power of Music," where Wesley asserts that things like counterpoint and harmony do not add to the goal of building up the affections and hence should be avoided (766–69). Regardless of the truth of such pronouncements, his single-mindedness regarding the affections is nonetheless apparent.

her family, etc., then we could fairly draw the conclusion that this was a man who loved his wife. One can have an emotion without constantly feeling it.

As Marshall might say, different things might "occasion" the feeling of an emotion, but the emotion itself is not exhaustively defined by those feelings. The emotion is the judgment or construal that has a particular history and takes certain features of reality as its objects (and typically disposes people to behave in a certain way, as shown below).

At a certain point in one of his justly famous sermon series, the contemporary minister Bishop T. D. Jakes, who has been dubbed "America's preacher" by *Time* magazine, contrasts a "churchy feeling" with a "true worship experience."[23] While he begins by trying to describe the different ways these "feelings" are experienced, in the end he has to resort to classical object-describing analyses, that is, true worship is focused on God. I think this contemporary example shows that while what we are experiencing as Christians is important, if we are counting on the experiential character of the sensation itself to describe what is key about our heart life, we will be in hard straits. Now, as in Wesley's time, we need a narrative description of the object of our attention, and that is given by the Church in her understanding of God as Trinity—Father, Son, and Holy Spirit.

Our heart life might be, in the words of the rock group Boston, "More Than a Feeling," but we need a narrative of our object if we are to correctly narrate just what that "more" is. There is an ancient Chinese proverb that says, "a picture is worth 10,000 words." I think that is true, but only if one *already knows* the 10,000 words. I think we have seen that the same is true for emotions—they can only be understood with the help of words—sometimes many, (perhaps not 10,000!), but a feeling by itself does not get us very far. This is the logic I see in Wesley's use of affection and feeling language.

23. "The Secret Place," a CD series published by T. D. Jakes Ministry, Dallas, Texas. See disc one, "Devil, You Can't Stop This," track 6.

5   Wesley's *Orthokardia*: The Genesis and *Telos* of the Affections

Here I want to gather together different expressions of Wesley's thought that illustrate how he understood the process of the formation and expression of affections. This could be understood as laying bare his *Orthokardia*—his vision of the right heart.[1] In doing this I will show Wesley thinks emotions are generated—specifically, whether or not he sees them as object- and judgment-related as the best contemporary theorists of Chapter Three discussed. Having shown the evidence for this, I will show whether Wesley saw the affections as necessarily expressing themselves in the actions of the believer—i.e., acting as dispositions to behave. If we can see these aspects of emotional logic or grammar, then Wesley might be seen as a worthy mentor and guide to Christian theology and practical application, the theme of part III of this text.

The Genesis of Affections—Affections as Object-related

As we have seen in the Chapter Three, contemporary theorists see the affections as being generated by taking certain objects, objects that often depend on a narrative for their description. Let us see if Wesley's views reflect this "transitive" or object-directed understanding. We will start with a phrase familiar to readers of Wesley's works, the "spiritual senses."

---

1. On this term *Orthokardia*, a neologism I created to describe Wesley's theologically normative vision of the heart, see my "*Orthokardia*."

The "Spiritual Senses"

For Wesley, there is an undeniable connection between the heart and the senses. On Eph 4:18 he commented: "Through the hardness of their hearts—Callous and senseless. And where there is no sense, there can be no life." On Mark 6:52 he says "Their heart was hardened—And yet they were not reprobates. It means only, they were slow and dull of apprehension." His emphasis on the senses led him to see that the "spiritual senses" were a necessary prerequisite for the development of the affections of the heart.

This might lead one to think that the "spiritual senses" should be seen as an important element of his "experimental" (experiential) approach to theology. The way it functions in his work, however, is as a hypothesized faculty or organ whose existence can only be inferred from the actual presence of the religious affections. As in most things, Wesley worked from the most real, obvious and concrete to the more abstract—if indeed it served some purpose to talk about abstractions at all![2] Let us consider some examples of his use of "spiritual sense" language from the *Notes*.

Matthew 13:14 and Wesley's comment on it reads "Hearing ye will hear, but in no wise understand—That is, ye will surely hear; all possible means will be given you; yet they will profit you nothing, because your heart is sensual, stupid, and insensible; your spiritual senses are shut up;

---

2. Rex Matthews in his article "With the Eyes of Faith," points-out that "spiritual experience" received through the "spiritual sense" is one of the three meanings of "faith" for Wesley, along with faith as belief and faith as trust. I agree with this, and I also agree with Frederick Dreyer's evaluation that the spiritual sense is an important aspect of Wesley's thought (see his "Faith and Experience in the Thought of John Wesley"). This does not contradict, however, my observation that this "sense" plays only a limited role in Wesley's thought. Matthews in his paper reinforces the textual evidence I share here to show that Wesley did not spend a lot of time elaborating this theory of the "spiritual sense." However, we need not necessarily conclude that Wesley derived this "sense" language primarily from the empiricism of Locke and Peter Browne (as Dreyer does). Richard Brantley in his *Locke, Wesley, and the Method of English Romanticism*, seems to make this association as well. Terrence Erdt in his "Calvinist Psychology of the Heart and the 'Sense' of Jonathan Edwards," has shown that Perry Miller and others who made similar claims about Jonathan Edwards and empiricism ignored the large body of puritan divinity that speaks about the "sense" of the heart and which was written many years before Locke was born. I think the same argument can be made regarding Wesley and empiricism *mutatis mutandis*.

yea, you have closed your eyes against the light. . . ." Along the same lines is Phil 1:9–10:

> In knowledge and in all spiritual sense— Which is the ground of all spiritual knowledge. We must be inwardly sensible of divine peace, joy, love; otherwise we cannot know what they are. [verse] 10. That ye may try—By that spiritual sense. The things that are excellent—Not only good, but the very best; the superior excellence of which is hardly discerned, but by the adult Christian.

Similar is 1 John 1:5 "That God is light—The light of wisdom, love, holiness, glory. What light is to the natural eye, that God is to the spiritual eye." A final example of this kind of discourse comes from Jude 1:10: "But these—Without all shame. Rail at the things [of God] which they know not—Neither can know, having no spiritual senses. And the natural things, which they know—By their natural senses, they abuse into occasions of sin."

These passages show the "spiritual sense" to be no mystical illative capacity or an arcane window into the mists of eternity granted only to the masters of the inner life, but something present in every simple believer. While the first and last quotes do speak of the spiritual senses in a substantial, if somewhat vague, way, the middle two quotes give a more explicit picture of what Wesley is trying to convey. Here it turns out that the spiritual sense is inextricably related to such everyday Christian emotions as peace, joy, and love. What this means is that to be filled with love of God, for example, is to have an awareness, a correct knowledge, of that spiritual reality known as "God." To be "inwardly sensible" of this love is to have a spiritual sense. This "sense" is nothing but a construct which is assumed to lie behind the affection. Wesley did not need to make many references to this sense because it is the first order realities (the affections) that he is trying to propagate among his readers, not a speculative, theoretical understanding of the believer's psychic make-up.[3]

3. On the topic of how "spiritual senses" have been understood in the Christian tradition, see Elizabeth Dryer's *Passionate Spirituality*, esp. chapter 2, "Passion in the Christian Tradition," where she references the work of, among others, Bernard McGinn, Karl Rahner, and Hans Urs von Balthasar. I see Randy Maddox as endorsing my metaphysically minimalist reading of Wesley's use of the term, seen especially in his reference to Nancey Murphy's "Non-reductive Physicalist Account of Religious Experience." Maddox's reference is found in his essay "Change in Affections."

This discussion leads us to the elusive and often misunderstood discussion about what is "inner" and what is "outer" in Wesley's vision of Christianity.

The "Inner" and the "Outer"

In a few places in the *N.T. Notes,* Wesley interpreted "sincerity" to be a cipher for the whole of the heart's affections: "Sincerity and truth seem to be put here for the whole of true, inward religion" (1 Cor 5:8). But this usage was relatively infrequent, probably because it sounds as if anything honestly "felt" (held, believed) would qualify as "true religion." Such would hardly be acceptable to Wesley, since Christianity is a specific, contingent pattern of affectivity that also has logical connections outside of the self to God and the world.

There are many cases where Wesley joins together in the same sentence references to both the inner world and the outer world. On Luke 15:31 he speaks about making progress "in inward as well as outward holiness." His note on 2 Cor 7:1 reads "Let us cleanse ourselves . . . from all pollution of the flesh—All outward sin. And of the spirit—All inward." The linkage is seen again in his comment on Rom 1:25: "And worshipped—Inwardly. And served—Outwardly."

A slight variation on this theme is seen in those passages where he links the inner and the outer, and emphasizes graphically that the outward aspect of religion alone is not enough. Commenting on Luke 11:44 Wesley mentions that "On another occasion Christ compared them to 'whited sepulchres,' fair without, but foul within (Matt. 23.27)." A similar comment appears on Acts 23:3: "God is about to smite thee, thou whited wall—Fair without; full of dirt and rubbish within."

His view becomes even clearer when we see that not only was outward religion not enough, but that inward religion has a logical priority over the outer. "My kingdom is not of this world—Is not an external, but a spiritual kingdom" (John 18:36). Again this is seen in Matt 7:15: "Beware of false prophets . . . in sheep's clothing— With outside religion, and fair professions of love"; and most clearly in the note to 1 Tim 2:2: "Godliness—Inward religion; the true worship of God."

But while there were, for Wesley, some legitimate uses of the inner/outer distinction regarding the proper Christian life, the distinction could not be over-arching or systematically universal, for in a very real sense the Christian affections are "outer" as well as inner. This is true in two senses. First, the affections arise from the person being directed, focused, fixed on some object. It is this object, coming to us from outside of our inner awareness, which is in many ways the cause of the affection. Secondly (as I will discuss below), Wesley sees affections as disposing us to actions in the world. In short, if affections are truly and completely "inner" they are not truly "religious."

The Transitivity of Emotion

The *N.T. Notes* are full of references to the fact that emotions take objects and that, specifically, the Christian emotions take God, and what God has done for us, as their object. In Rom 1:4 we read, "By the resurrection from the dead—For this is both the foundation and the object of our faith; and the preaching of the apostles was the consequence of Christ's resurrection." In Luke 11:33, "The meaning is, God gives you this gospel light, that you may repent. Let your eye be singly fixed on Him, aim only at pleasing God; and while you do this, your whole soul will be full of wisdom, holiness, and happiness." On Rom 1:7 he says, "Our trust and prayer fix on God, as He is the Father of Christ; and on Christ, as He presents us to the Father." Later in Romans we see, "If we believe on Him who raised up Jesus—God the Father is therefore the proper object of justifying faith" (Rom 4:24).

That specific affections find their genesis in this way is shown in Wesley's comment on Rom 1:21: "They did not glorify him as God, neither were thankful—They neither thanked Him for His benefits, nor glorified Him for His divine perfections." Here we see that our thankfulness to God comes from targeting what God has done for us. In the same way, our praise or glorification of God takes God's perfections as its object.

His comment on 2 Cor 5:13 shows us that even in religious ecstasies, the Christian is not an idiot (in the Greek sense of *idios*—"one's own") but is still fixed on God:

> For if we are transported beyond ourselves—Or, at least, appear
> so to others, treated of verses 15–21, speaking or writing with un-
> common vehemences. It is to God—He understands (if men do
> not) the emotion which Himself inspires.

Such experiences, if genuine, are not the novel creation of unbalanced
people, they are simply the result of realizing who God is and what God
has done.

The transitivity of emotion, of course, does not apply only to the religious affections, but also to the natural affections:

> They that are after the flesh . . . mind the things of the flesh—Have
> their thoughts and affections fixed on such things as gratify cor-
> rupt nature: namely, on things visible and temporal: on things of
> the earth, on pleasure (of sense or imagination), praise, or riches.
> But they who are after the Spirit—Who are under His guidance.
> Mind the things of the Spirit—Think of, relish, love things invis-
> ible, eternal; the things which the Spirit hath revealed, which He
> works in us, moves us to, and promises to give us. (Rom 8:5)

Whatever is the object of our attention will determine the form of our
heart, the posture of our soul, the nature of our affections. In the words of
the scripture text Matt 6:21–23:

> For where your treasure is, there will your heart be also. The eye
> is the lamp of the body: if therefore thine eye be single, thy whole
> body shall be full of light. But if thine eye be evil, thy whole body
> shall be full of darkness.[4]

---

4. In the 1998 national meeting of the Academy of Religion, Dr. Owen Thomas
presented a paper to the Christian Spirituality group entitled "Interiority and Christian
Spirituality," subsequently published with the same title in *The Journal of Religion*. In
this paper he claims that the long Christian tradition of emphasizing the "interior" life is
mistaken, and that we should move to an emphasis "on the outer as primary and a major
source of the inner." I think what he was after is addressed in this object-centered emphasis of Wesley on the affections. See also Bernard McGinn's essay "Language of Inner
Experience in Christian Mysticism," where he makes clear how problematic a simple
understanding of "inner experience" can be.

Interpretive Problems Avoided in Light of Wesley's Object-related Heart Religion

Failing to understand this transitive nature of Wesley's view of affectivity can lead to serious interpretive problems. This can be seen in John Deschner's analysis of *Wesley's Christology*.[5] In the 1985 foreword to the reprint edition of this book, Deschner states clearly the importance and contemporary relevance of Wesley's soteriological formulations. Deschner points out that, for Wesley, salvation is a "present thing" and that the mind of Christ

> takes form today in the renewed 'affections' of the believer's heart—those affections which constitute the presence in the forgiven sinner of the progressively recovered image of *God. . . . this* is the Christological foundation of the Methodist tradition and the main emphasis in any Methodist contribution to the ecumenical recovery of the wholeness of the apostolic faith.[6]

But after this glowing endorsement of Wesley's emphasis on the affections in the foreword, later, in the body of the text, Deschner launches a critique of Wesley that betrays a misunderstanding of Wesley's conception of the affections. Part of Deschner's critique of Wesley is that the moral law given in the Old Testament retains a "semi-independence from Christ."[7] Even when it is understood that for Wesley love is the sum of the law, Deschner still objects that

> [Wesley] means by love, not primarily participation in the being of Christ's love, but an inherent 'temper', 'affection' or 'intention' in man, himself. . . . the independence of the love demanded from the holiness of Christ's active obedience is the root of a far-reaching question about the justice of man's final justification.[8]

Deschner is concerned that Wesley's understanding of holiness is too easily translated into a legalistic moralism, depending on subjective feelings and one's own will to get to heaven. That this understanding was indeed adopted by some of Wesley's followers (especially in the nineteenth

5. Deschner, *Christology*.

6. Ibid., xvi–xvii.

7. Ibid., 106. See also 107–8; 140–41; 154ff.; 180; 193f.

8. Ibid., 106.

century) is undeniable, but it is not fair to accuse Wesley of this. On this point, Deschner seems to have seen Schleiermacher when he looked at Wesley, which is understandable since Deschner originally wrote his book as a dissertation under the direction of Karl Barth, the great critic of Schleiermacher. The key words in the above quote that betray Deschner's misunderstanding of Wesley's view of the affections are "inherent" and "independent."

We have seen that for Wesley the affections are not "inherent" and "independent," but are causally dependent on targeting the "things of God," taking the gospel as the object of our attention, centering our hearts and minds on what God has done for us. We love, not because we have some "inherent" and "independent" principle inside of us. We love because God first loved us. This is no Schleiermacherian in-built "feeling of absolute dependence"; it is a contingent pattern of affectivity, it is the result of being formed in the Christian rule of life. Holiness is not a question of autonomous willing guided by inherent principles or spontaneous and unpredictable up-wellings of intense feeling, it is "righteousness, joy and peace *in the Holy Ghost.*"[9]

The gracious affections, then, are not mere sensations but are analyzable, cognitively charged responses to certain objects, especially God's atoning work in Christ. Animated in the synergism of the Holy Spirit and the human spirit, they pattern and orient the self. As we will see in detail below, through the confirmation and strengthening of the sacramental ministry of the church, these become dispositions to behave, dispositions to do those works of love and mercy that the compassionate heart perceives to be needed.

9. Romans 14:17, one of Wesley's favorite descriptions of the Kingdom of God. Geoffrey Wainwright also criticizes Deschner for denying that holiness is achieved on Wesley's terms by "participating in Christ," though Wainwright does so by emphasizing Wesley's sacramental views. I agree with Wainwright's sacramental point, but I think Deschner's more fundamental confusion lies in his understanding of Wesley's view of the affections. See Wainwright's Review of *Wesley's Christology*. On the question of Wesley's understanding of the law, see Leander Keck's *Paul and His Letters*, and Krister Stendahl's *Paul Among Jews and Gentiles*, for discussions of Paul's understanding of the law. It seems that if one accepts the analysis of Paul's views of the law as set forth by Keck and Stendahl (i.e., that the law itself is not bad, but that it can not bring about what only faith can do) then Wesley's claims that the "law is established through faith" and that "faith is the handmaid to love" (see sermons 35 and 36, especially *Works*, 2:38) are perhaps more Pauline than some Reformation understandings.

The transitive (and dispositional) nature of the affections is seen consistently throughout Wesley's works, and I think this definite pattern of logical connections outside of the self supports the judgment that Wesley's conception of the religious affections is "rational." Another way of approaching the question of the "rationality" of these affections is to ask the question: Does the object under consideration *justify* the emotion elicited? This question cannot be answered in the abstract but only within a particular context in a particular community.

Fear of trolls is irrational in societies which consider such beasts non-existent. Love of God is irrational if one believes that God does not exist. Unbelievers, therefore, might find Wesley's whole scheme to be irrational because of their very unbelief in God. But since, presumably, unbelievers would find *any* portrayal of Christian theology to be irrational, their rejection of Wesley's theology would not be a telling critique of his specifically affection-centered theology.[10]

Why Renewing the Heart Can only Take Place in Community

Understanding the proper end, goal, or telos of the properly shaped heart was a major focus of Wesley's theology. In this section I will show how the "dispositional" nature of the affections can be seen in his work.

Society and the Affections

Religious affections, then, are not totally self-contained "inner" realities in that they require an object. Their generation is a result of the soul turning to God. If God is not the object, they are not Christian affections. But this is not the only outward-turning aspect of Christian emotion.

That Wesley himself constantly did good works is well known to all who have studied his life, and this emphasis on works is also found in the *N.T. Notes*. Commenting on Jas 2:14, Wesley notes that the book of "James refutes not the doctrine of St. Paul, but the error of those who abused it." He later specifies this by saying, "Works do not give life to

10. For a discussion of how "reason" requires a specific community, see the work of Alasdair MacIntyre, especially *Whose Justice? Which Rationality?* 25.

faith, but faith begets works, and then is perfected by them" (Jas 2:22). On Acts 27:23 we read, "The God whose I am, and whom I serve—How short a compendium of religion! yet how full! comprehending faith, hope, and love!"

The same theme is seen in Matt 7:16:

> By their fruits ye shall know them—A short, plain, easy rule, whereby to know true from false prophets; and one that may be applied by people of the meanest capacity, who are not accustomed to deep reasoning. True prophets convert sinners to God, or at least confirm and strengthen those that are converted. False prophets do not.

This responsibility to be active in the world is also implied in Wesley's comment on John 2:2: "Jesus and his disciples were invited to the marriage—Christ does not take away human society, but sanctifies it."

What may not be as widely recognized as Wesley's emphasis on works is that, on Wesley's terms, these works are to issue from those affections and tempers which come from targeting God with our attention: "He that soweth sparingly shall reap sparingly; he that soweth bountifully shall reap bountifully—A general rule. God will proportion the reward to the work, *and the temper whence it proceeds*" (2 Cor 9:6; emphasis mine). In commenting on Matt 6:1, he says that this chapter is about "the purity of intention without which none of our outward actions are holy." Where Jas 1:26 reads, "Pure religion and undefiled before God even the Father is this, To visit the fatherless and widows in their affliction, and to keep himself unspotted from the world," Wesley comments "But this cannot be done till we have given our hearts to God, and love our neighbor as ourselves."

On this point it should be recalled what Wesley said in his comment on 1 Thess 2:17. There he wrote about the "calm standing tempers, that fixed posture of the soul" that is the distinguishing sign of the human character. It is the opposite of such dispositions that characterizes the wicked man: "So changeable are the hearts of wicked men! So little are their starts of love to be depended on!" (Luke 4:28). Only the Christian affections yield the fruits that persevere.

Thus the telos, like the genesis, of the affections lies outside of the self. In this sense also, then, the religious affections are not a purely "inner" phenomena. Or, we might say, if they are only inner, then they are not really religious. To love God and one's neighbor, to take joy in the happiness of others, to fear the wrath of God, all imply dispositions to behave in certain ways. We do not seek to serve our neighbor because of some inherent attractiveness of the neighbor, but because of who God is, what God has done for us, and the consequent love and gratitude which are generated in us by these realities.[11] Just as the quality of the object determined whether the affection was truly religious, so the quality of the resulting action is an indicator of the nature of the affection. Though one cannot know the state of the heart *only* by looking at the outward person, the behavior or action ("fruits") of the person is one important indicator of the purity of the heart.

Self-Deception and the Affections

There are many examples of self-deception in the New Testament and Wesley is eager to put them to didactic use. On Col 2:18 he shows that what was thought to be humility was really pride; on Luke 13:16 he points out that the real motive involved was envy and not "pure zeal for the glory of God"; on Luke 16:3 he quotes an uncited source that recognized this tendency to produce deluded evaluations of the self and its motives and affections: "By men called honour, but by angels pride." Even the proceedings of the historical Church councils, when they took the form of anathemas, "consecrated some of the most devilish passions under the most sacred names; and, like some ill-adjusted weapons of war, are most likely to hurt the hand from which they are thrown" (Acts 15:29).

Humans being what they are, there can be no once and for all remedies for this tendency, but Wesley does recommend several safeguards. The most general and most important of these comes, not surprisingly, from the pattern set by Christ. In this case, what he is singling out from Christ's life for imitation is the self-denial symbolized in the cross.

Where Matthew states, "Let him deny himself, and take up his cross," Wesley comments, "A rule that can never be too much observed: let him in all things deny his own will, however pleasing, and do the will of God,

11. On this theme of relating to our neighbors through God, compare Augustine's *On Christian Doctrine* 1.32: "The greatest reward is that we enjoy Him and that all of us who enjoy Him may enjoy one another in Him" (Robertson, 28).

however painful" (Matt 16:24). Shortly after this same passage appears in Luke, Wesley writes, "In joy remember the cross. So wisely does our Lord balance praise with sufferings" (Luke 9:44).

Aside from this general admonition, Wesley gives several other specific checks against self-deception in the course of his exposition of the New Testament. One most frequently mentioned is Scripture itself. The charge to "try the spirits" is understood by Wesley to mean "We are to try all spirits by the written word: 'To the law and the testimony!' If any man speak not according to these, the spirit which actuates him is not of God" (1 John 4:1). Similarly, "prove all things" means "Try every advice by the touchstone of Scripture . . ." (1 Thess 5:21).

Other checks to delusion are the reproof of others (Matt 18:15), the passage of time (Matt 13:26), and, most importantly, the person's own actions. As shown above, the religious affections imply certain actions in the world, the society of others, and if these dispositions are not present, as shown through good works, then the affections under scrutiny are not in fact Christian. If we shut up our compassion to our brother or sister in need, does God dwell in our hearts? "Certainly not at all, however he may talk (verse 18) of loving God" (1 John 3:17).

Thus the dispositional nature of the affections is the ultimate check against self-deception. This fact, along with the transitive and rational nature of the affections, can all be seen in Wesley's note to Phil 1:10–11. This can serve nicely as a summary statement of the grammar of the religious affections.

> That ye may be inwardly sincere—Having a single eye to the very best of things, and a pure heart. And outwardly without offense— Holy, unblamable in all things.
>
> v. 11 Being filled with the fruits of righteousness, which are through Jesus Christ, to the glory and praise of God—Here are three properties of that sincerity which is acceptable to God: (1) It must bear fruits, the fruits of righteousness, all inward and outward holiness, all good tempers, words, and works; and that so abundantly that we may be filled with them. (2) The branch and the fruits must derive both their virtue and their very being from the all-supporting, all-supplying root, Jesus Christ. (3) As all these flow from the grace of Christ, so they must issue in the glory and praise of God.

The related problems of idolatry and self-deception are dealt with at length in several of Wesley's sermons as well, especially number 37, "The Nature of Enthusiasm." Here, Wesley says that if one performs a round of outward duties, asserts orthodox opinions and exhibits a certain quantity of "heathen morality" then people will consider such a person within the bounds of acceptability. "But if you aim at the religion of the heart, if you talk of 'righteousness, and peace, and joy in the Holy Ghost', then it will not be long before your sentence is passed, 'Thou art beside thyself'" (#37, 46). But it was so important to attain to this "righteousness, peace and joy" that Wesley ran the risk of being called an enthusiast and in this sermon he set out his own counter-attacking notion of what enthusiasm really is.

The part of this sermon most pertinent to our concern with the affections is the passage where he speaks about knowing the will of God. How are we to know this?

> Not by waiting for supernatural dreams; not by expecting God to reveal it in visions; not by looking for any *particular impressions* [emphasis his] or sudden impulses on his mind: no; but by consulting the oracles of God. 'To the law and to the testimony!' This is the general method of knowing what is 'the holy and acceptable will of God.' (#37, 54)

Here we again see, as we previously noted in our discussion of his *N.T. Notes*, Wesley warning against a retreat to subjectivity for guidance in our spiritual life. In the sermons, Wesley emphasizes the object-related and action-disposing "affections" over against the narrow awareness-of-sensation that we associate with the term "feeling."[12]

Works and the Heart

Wesley's writings show us that his emphasis on the religious affections as the "marks of the new birth" is precisely what led him into the world of action and society, not something that tempted him away from it. The conceptual linkage between a right heart and right works, in fact, moves

---

12. For other references to objective, external, checks on our spiritual life, see number 65 "The Duty of Reproving Our Neighbor." On humility and repentance as checks on our emotions, see number 48 "Self-Denial."

in both directions: right works require a right heart and a right heart requires right works.

That "right works require a right heart" is seen throughout the sermons. Even in the first sermon of the corpus, "Salvation by Faith," we read that "Only corrupt fruit grows on a corrupt tree" (#1, 118). Discourse six on the Sermon on the Mount (number 26) is concerned to show "how all our actions likewise, even those that are indifferent in their own nature, may be made holy and good and acceptable to God, by a pure and holy intention. Whatever is done without this, he largely declares, is of no value before God" (#26, 573). Again in "On Perfection" we see that "Holiness of life" arises from "holiness of heart" (#76, 75). This is stated most starkly, perhaps, in number 7, "The Way to the Kingdom":

> Yea, two persons may do the same outward work-suppose, feeding the hungry, or clothing the naked and in the meantime one of these may be truly religious and the other have no religion at all; for the one may act from the love of God, and the other from the love of praise. So manifest is it that although true religion naturally leads to every good word and work, yet the real nature thereof lies deeper still, even in 'the hidden man of the heart.' (#7, 220)

Similarly, that a right heart requires right works is equally plain in the sermons. The most extended attention to this topic is sermon 24, the fourth discourse on the Sermon on the Mount. Here he begins by saying "The beauty of holiness, of that inward man of the heart which is renewed after the image of God, cannot but strike every eye which God hath opened, every enlightened understanding" (#24, 531). Shortly after this he states:

> If religion therefore were carried no farther than this they could have no doubt concerning it—they should have no objection against pursuing it with the whole ardour of their souls. But why, say they, is it clogged with other things? What need of loading it with *doing* and *suffering?* These are what damps the vigor of the soul and sinks it down to earth again. Is it not enough to 'follow after charity'? To soar upon the wings of love? Will it not suffice to worship God, who is a Spirit, with the spirit of our minds, without encumbering ourselves with outward things, or even thinking of them at all? (#24, 531–32, emphasis his)

The answer to this is, of course, that "Christianity is essentially a social religion, and that to turn it into a solitary one is to destroy it; secondly, that to conceal this religion is impossible, as well as utterly contrary to the design of its author" (#24, 533). Explaining this he says "Ye may not flee from men, and while ye are among them it is impossible to hide your lowliness and meekness and those dispositions whereby ye aspire to be perfect, as your Father in heaven is perfect. Love cannot be hid any more than light; and least of all when it shines forth in action . . . (#24, 539). While it is true that the "root of religion lies in the heart," it is also true that such a root "cannot but put forth branches" (#24,541).

One of the clearest examples of a failure to act that damages the affections is in not giving all one can. In sermon 87, "The Danger of Riches," he sets forth his famous dictum, "Gain all you can, save all you can, give all you can," and he also states there that riches allow us to gratify foolish desires that lead to "unholy desires, and every unholy passion and temper. We easily pass from these to pride, anger, bitterness, envy, malice, revengefulness; to an headstrong, unadvisable spirit—indeed, to every temper that is earthly, sensual, or devilish" (#87, 236). This same theme is seen in 108, "On Riches," as well as 122, "Causes of the Inefficacy of Christianity." In this last, he shows his increasing unhappiness over how his Methodists are handling their growing prosperity:

> . . . you may find many that observe the First rule, namely, 'Gain all you can.' You may find a few that observe the Second, 'Save all you can:' But how many have you found that observe the Third rule, 'Give all you can?' Have you reason to believe that five hundred of these are to be found among fifty thousand Methodists? And yet nothing can be more plain, than that all who observe the two first rules without the third, will be twofold more the children of hell than ever were before. (#122, 91)

So firmly did Wesley hold that embodying the Christian affections was the key point in being a Christian that in a letter of June 30, 1743, to his sister Emilia he warned her that her lack of thankfulness to God and man rendered her as much a sinner as "whores and murderers."[13] Placing the central emphasis on the disposition of the heart allowed Wesley to be tolerant with regard to most of those issues that many contentious

---

13. *Works*, 26:100.

Christians staked their whole identity on. To Mrs. Howton in October of 1783, he wrote, "It is the glory of the people called Methodists that they condemn none for their opinions or modes of worship. They think and let think, and insist upon nothing but faith working by love."[14]

Writing to "John Smith," Wesley shows clearly the priority of love in the hierarchy of the affections:

> I would just add that I regard even faith itself not as an *end,* but a *means* only. The end of the commandment is love—of every command, of the whole Christian dispensation. Let this love be attained, by whatever means, and I am content; I desire no more. All is well if we love the Lord our God with all our heart, and our neighbor as ourselves.[15]

Even the role of the church is ultimately defined in relation to the affections for Wesley. Again to "John Smith" Wesley asks, "'What is the end of all ecclesiastical order?' Is it not to bring souls from the power of Satan to God, and to build them up in his fear and love? Order, then, is so far valuable as it answers these ends: and if it answers them not, it is nothing worth."[16]

Conclusions: Wesley's Heart Religion in Evaluative Overview[17]

In light of this analysis it is perhaps easy to understand how some interpreters of Wesley's heart religion, like Richard B. Steele, see it in the "voluntarist" tradition,[18] while others, like D. Stephen Long, see it as part

14. *Letters*, Telford, ed., 7:190. See also his sermon, "The Way to the Kingdom" (#7, 220), and "The Character of a Methodist," *Works* 9:34.

15. Letter of June 25, 1746, *Works*, 26:203.

16. Letter of June 25, 1746, *Works*, 26:206.

17. A nice summary of Wesley's views on the "grammar" of the heart and the role of affectivity in the Christian life is found in his abridgment and publication of Jonathan Edwards's *Treatise on Religious Affections*. In this work one can find all of the themes I have emphasized in this chapter. Those who want to pursue this can consult a number of recent publications See not only my *John Wesley on Religious Affections*, chapter 6, "True Religion and the Affections," but also Steele's *"Gracious Affections" and "True Virtue"*, as well as Kevin Lowery's *Salvaging Wesley's Agenda*, esp. chapter 6, "The Cognitive Contents of Emotions."

18. See Steele, *"Gracious Affections" and "True Virtue"*, esp. chapter 2, "Reason, Virtue

of the "intellectualist" stream of thought.[19] Voluntarism sees the will, in one way or another, as more basic than intellect, while intellectualists (like Aquinas, whom Long champions as an ally of Wesley) see the will as a "rational appetite" that follows the last dictate of the intellect. But if we see that Wesley meant nothing more by "will" than the affections,[20] then we have at the pulsating center of "will" both reasoning judgments or construals and (often) felt realities. Wesley's understanding of the nature of affectivity makes him hard to classify in these categories: if we focus on passages that oppose "affections" to "cold or speculative "reason" then he sounds like a voluntarist; if, on the other hand, we focus on those passages that emphasize the cognitive component of the affections, he sounds like an intellectualist.[21]

This is similar to another, more common, problem with characterizing Wesley's heart religion. Paul Chilcote, in his fine study of both John and Charles, emphasizes that the Wesleys refused to be "disjunctive" theologians in favor of being "conjunctive" theologians.[22] One of the "conjunctions" that Chilcote addresses as a common disjunction is "head" and "heart." While Chilcote's seeing these two elements as brought together in Wesley's thought could be construed as consistent with my analysis, it is also possible to assume, given the distinctions implied by theses two

and Affectivity in the Voluntarist Tradition."

19. See Long, *John Wesley's Moral Theology*. Significantly, Long, a student of Stanley Hauerwas, prefers "virtue" language to "temper" or "affection" language. See 140, and his Appendix B, "Wesley's Holy Tempers: The Theological Virtues."

20. See, for example, "Of Good Angels" where he says ". . . the affections are only the will exerting itself in various ways . . ." (#71, 6). Compare this with "Thoughts Upon Necessity," where Wesley states, "It seems, they who divide the faculties of the human soul into the understanding, will, and affections, unless they make the will and affections the same thing; (and then how inaccurate is the division!) must mean by affections, the will, properly speaking, and by the term will, neither more nor less than liberty; the power of choosing either to do or not to do, (commonly called liberty of contradiction,) or to do this or the contrary, good or evil (commonly called liberty of contrariety)" (Jackson *Works*, 10:468–69).

21. Though Long acknowledges that Wesley, at times, sounds like a voluntarist, especially when Wesley puts the faculty of "liberty" as more basic than the will, Long sees this as "deleterious" and leading to internal contradictions in Wesley's thought. See 43ff. and 64–65. Long wants to promote a reading of Wesley as consistent with Aquinas on this issue, which means downplaying the "voluntarist" tendencies of Wesley.

22. See his *Recapturing the Wesley's Vision*, especially his preface and introduction, and chapter 5, "Holistic Formation (Instruction) Heart and Head."

separate terms, that when Wesley brought these two into conjunction that there was no previous cognitive component in the "heart" that was brought to the conjunction with the "head." What I hope to have demonstrated in my analysis is that when we understand what Wesley meant by the affections, we see that the split between head and heart was never there to begin with—the affections have their own cognitive component and don't need another stage in mental integration in order to be linked to either the senses or the intellect.

In his *The Making of the English Working Class,* E. P. Thompson called Methodism "a ritualized form of psychic masturbation."[23] In point of fact, Wesley did once write a pamphlet on the very subject of "Onanism." A quote from Wesley is also listed in the *Oxford English Dictionary* under the listing for the word "Enthusiast."[24] But in both the pamphlet and the quote in the *O.E.D.,* Wesley not only recognizes the possibility and reality of self-manipulation, but he also warns against it. This vigilance against "curving in on oneself" (to use Luther's phrase) is never more apparent than when Wesley speaks about the affections.

As we have seen, Wesley does not recommend a religion of sheer undifferentiated feeling. What makes an affection Christian (or "religious" or "gracious") is the object which engenders it. To be specific, the genuine religious affections take as their object the God presented in the biblical stories of the Jews and Jesus, the Messiah. Having such a "descriptive" object as the target of our affections is admittedly different than having them take a spatio-temporal object like a tree or a human being but, as we have seen in chapter 3, a descriptive narrative of the object is typically a part of *any* emotion/affection.

This object-centeredness, of course, can open-up another possibility for delusion, namely taking the *wrong* description of God as the object of the affections. As Wesley well knew, you will have a different affectional make-up if you think God is cruel, indifferent or an abstract "first principle." But Wesley's constant insistence on the normative nature of Scripture (especially as historically interpreted by the Church) as the main source for our understanding of both God and ourselves is another very strong check against tailoring our religion to our own desires, fears, or whatever spirit is prevailing in our particular age.

23. *Making of the English Working Class, 368.*
24. See *OED,* 1:876.

Since our focus in this chapter has been on what Wesley *said* in his published works about the affections, we have not considered what shape the actual *practice* of his own ministry took in forming these affections in his scattered flocks. But it must not be forgotten, especially when considering the problem of self-deception, that one of the most important instruments that Wesley used for deepening the faith, hope and love of believers was the class meeting. Wesley was not one to recommend lonely mountaintop contemplation, for he knew too well the human heart's propensity for deceit. Wesley was constantly forming new believers into classes, societies and bands where the Christians could examine each other and openly and honestly share with each other the course of their spiritual struggles. Seeking "feedback" and direction from others was more the norm for the Methodist movement than the exception. Wesley's emphasis on the social nature of the Christian life and the constant need to guard against self-deception—in other words, the need for "accountable discipleship"—has been very helpfully expounded in David Lowes Watson's book *The Early Methodist Class Meeting.*[25]

We have also seen that having a Christian "heart" logically entails the doing of certain actions in the world, summarized briefly as loving your neighbor. A right heart requires right works just as doing works Christianly requires a right heart. If Wesley had said that being a Christian meant only experiencing certain positive feelings, like pleasure, then he would be an appropriate patron saint of narcissism. But Wesley's understanding of Christianity called for self-denial, taking up one's cross and following after Christ. The love, joy and peace of this life are all marked by humility and the "filial fear" of offending God, and there is a continuing need for "The Repentance of Believers" (sermon number 14).

Wesley placed true religion in the realm of the affections, but to understand correctly what he means by this is to see that the grammar of the religious affections bursts open the self in two different ways. At their genesis, the affections are formed by attending to the work of Christ, which is not something self-generated but is something which comes to us as proclamation. After grace has thus led us to faith, we are naturally led to do the "works of mercy" by the love of God and neighbor which has

25. For two contemporary secular discussions of how a select "competent community" is necessary for effective interpretation, discussion and formation, see Wayne Booth's *Dogma of Modem Assent,* and Hans-Georg Gadamer's *Truth and Method.*

grown within us. Thus the affections have not only their genesis outside of the self, but their *telos* as well.[26]

On this understanding, then, Wesley escapes the critique of "religion as inwardness" which Dietrich Bonhoeffer levels in his writings.[27] We can now also see why Feuerbach's famous criticism of theologies like that of Schleiermacher cannot find root in Wesley's thought. For Wesley, it is not the feelings that are worshiped, but the object that engenders the emotion, and the emotions are not judged to be truly religious unless they issue in action.[28] There is no such thing as a solitary Christian for Wesley, and the Christian that does no works is no Christian at all. In The "Large Minutes" of the Methodist conference, the purpose of the group is set out as propagating scriptural holiness *and* reforming the nation, *not* one or the other, and we have seen how *both* actions flow from the renewed heart.[29]

We see in all of this, then, the answer not just to the question of self-deception as a spiritual problem, but also to the another critical question about "heart religion" that might be raised: whether or not an emphasis on the affections necessarily fosters a religion of extreme individualism. Doing works in society is ingredient in having a religious affection. Wesley's observation that "there can be no holiness but social holiness" is entirely consistent with his emphasis on the religious affections.

Moreover, Wesley's discussions of the affections, which, on the whole, reflect a careful balance of feeling, object and disposition, shed light on a paradox of which most of us are aware. The paradox I refer to is the fact that for some people, their most deeply held convictions are guarded by an outward calm, an apparent serenity, rather than strong displays of feeling. These convictions seem somehow too important, too deep, to all-encompassingly self-involving to try to display them in an episodically exuberant way. I think this is so because the dispositional nature of our emotions is seen most clearly in our strongest affections.

26. On the subtle temptation to target our feelings instead of targeting God, see C. S. Lewis's *Screwtape Letters*, letter number 6.

27. See *Letters and Papers from Prison*, letter of July 8, 1944.

28. The most concise summary of Ludwig's Feuerbach's views can be found in *Essence of Christianity*, and especially the foreword by H. Richard Niebuhr and introduction by Karl Barth in the Harper Torchbook version.

29. Jackson *Works*, 8:299.

The dispositional nature of our religious beliefs is so clear that to try to express them completely through bursts of feeling is clearly futile. Feeling just cannot be substituted for action. Wesley realized that what makes religious language so hard to speak is that it is an idiom which demands much of the speaker. The "meaning" of our religious discourse is not found in a feeling, but in the actions which make-up our lives.[30]

Freud and Marx showed that history—both personal and societal—can distort what we call "reason." Wittgenstein went beyond these insights and showed that in fact "reason" *required* history, that is, a pre-existing community of shared language and practice. Wittgenstein's insights into reason can be found *mutatis mutandis* in Wesley's insights into the religious affections. The affections require a society, a community, for both their formation and their expression. The church conveys the story of God's action and provides the liturgical means for forming the affections that the story engenders. And the church and the wider community are the arena for the actions to which the affections dispose the believers. The religious affections for Wesley were fundamentally relational.

Let us now turn to the normative theological question of how this vision of "heart religion," when understood correctly, might impact the Church today.

---

30. On this theme, see Saliers, *Soul in Paraphrase*, esp. 112ff. Saliers says that living out of certain emotions means more than having intense feelings but entails taking-up a way of life (113). For a criticism of substituting feeling for action, see Jean-Paul Sartre's *Emotions*. While Sartre has made a profound insight into some types of emotional experience, he unfortunately over-generalizes and can see no positive role for emotion, terming all emotion a degradation of consciousness.

PART III

The Joyful Work of Heart Renewal Today

6   Teaching for the Renewal of the Heart

Wesley's Heart Religion as a Truly Practical Theology[1]

This chapter will draw on what I have established in the previous chapters in order to show how doing theology in the tradition of Wesley today can be done with fidelity to his vision of "heart religion" as well as with intellectual, and theological, integrity—all while being truly "practical" in the best sense of that term. As a way to begin this process, I will start with the question: What makes Wesley's theological vision especially "practical?" Then, given the answer to that question, I want to explore how theology and spiritual formation should be taught in the Wesleyan tradition today. I will end by considering the question "Should those who want to promulgate a Wesleyan-style 'heart religion' relate to the essential Christian doctrines any differently than Wesley related to them in his day?"

What makes Wesley's Theological Vision "Practical?"

In Randy Maddox's *Responsible Grace* he states that Wesley's theology is a *practical* theology because it was about "nurturing and shaping the world-view that frames the temperament and practice of believer's lives in the world."[2] I agree with this way of putting it. In his article "John Wesley—Practical Theologian?" in the *Wesleyan Theological Journal* and in his article "The Recovery of Theology as a Practical Discipline" in *Theological*

---

1. Part of what follows is taken from a paper was originally presented to the Wesleyan Studies group of the national meeting of the American Academy of Religion held in Atlanta, Georgia, November 2003. A version of this paper was subsequently published as "Wesley's 'Main Doctrines,'" 97–121.

2. Maddox, *Responsible*, 16–17.

Studies, Maddox highlights this distinctive view in the course of narrating the history of theology from its church-and monastery-based beginnings to its eventual capture by the academic model of the universities and the resulting transformations for understanding "*practical*" theology.

In all of this, Maddox makes the case that Wesley was a practical theologian in that he thought theology *per se* should be practical, and that the appellation "practical theology" should not be reserved only for certain areas of applied or "pastoral" theology. On this point, Maddox's view of Wesley's theology is very similar to how Ellen Charry has portrayed theology in her book *By The Renewing of Our Minds*. This can be contrasted with understandings of "practical theology" that are typically encountered today that in fact might better be called *pastoral* theology as their focus is on pastoral functions such as preaching, pastoral care, worship, religious education, ministry, administration, and evangelism.[3]

Maddox asserts that a truly practical theology in this tradition should be marked by five characteristics: it should be transformative, holistic, recognize the primacy of practice, and be contextual and occasional.[4] In my view, the "transformative" and "holistic" dimensions of this paradigm are particularly applicable to Wesley's theology. What must be kept in view, though, and what is often ignored, is that Wesley expresses these dimensions *in the idiom of heart language*. In elaborating on what he means by holistic, Maddox makes explicit use of the "three ortho" pattern that Ted Runyon and I have used in different ways: seeing Christianity as being described not only in terms of orthodoxy—right beliefs, and orthopraxis—right action, but also in terms of *orthokardia* (my term) or *orthopathy* (Runyon's term)—the right heart.[5]

However, in considering this five-fold pattern for practical theology, we must be especially cautious when interpreting the criterion of the "primacy of practice." Given contemporary discussion of practice that could lead to distortions of Wesley's vision, we might better leave that out.

---

3. See Emory's website http://www.emory.edu/GDR/lillyinitiative.htm.

4. Maddox, "John Wesley—Practical Theologian?" 134–35.

5. I used this threefold pattern in my PhD dissertation, subsequently revised and published as my first book, *John Wesley on Religious Affections*, and Ted Runyon, who served on my dissertation committee, used this pattern in several places. See especially his *New Creation*.

Specifically, we cannot interpret Wesley as meaning that having a practical theology should put a primary emphasis on "practices."

Holiness and Practices[6]

The word "practice" has been increasingly current in the vocabulary in theologians in the last few years as seen in a number of publications including *Growing in the Life of Faith* (by Craig Dykstra, the head of the trend-setting Religion Division of the Lilly Endowment), *Practicing our Faith*,[7] and *Practicing Theology*.[8] Some of this flows from an appreciation of Alisdair MacIntyre's reflections,[9] but much can be traced to a related source—an appreciation for the work of George Lindbeck in his *The Nature of Doctrine*. In this book, Lindbeck offers the now-famous analysis that "religion" has typically been understood in one of three ways: either as doctrine, or as a kind of experience, or as a cultural-linguistic set of practices—a way of life.

Lindbeck's first understanding of religion-as-doctrine can be seen in "confessional" churches where a creed or confession—some set of rational propositions—is seen as defining who they are. The second understanding of religion as experience is exemplified in the theology of Schleiermacher who said that the essence of Christianity is the "feeling of absolute dependence." This view is also found in the thought of those who hold that the different religions are merely different "expressions" of one common and universally available experience. Related to, and informing, Lindbeck's third option are the works of such diverse people as Weber, Wittgenstein, and Geertz,[10] (though one could also easily draw parallels between the cultural-linguistic model and Kierkegaard's emphasis on Christianity as a lived reality, and not merely a speculative scheme[11]). All

---

6. Part of what follows in this section has been adapted from my essay "Shaping Heart Religion through Preaching and Pastoral Care" in the volume edited by Richard Steele, *"Heart Religion" in the Methodist Tradition and Related Movements*, 209–24.

7. Edited by Dorothy Bass.

8. Edited by Volf and Bass. See especially the essays by Volf, Jones, Pauw, Dykstra, and Bass.

9. See especially his *After Virtue*.

10. Lindbeck, *Nature*, 20.

11. See his *Concluding Unscientific Postscript*, among other works.

of these people associated with this third option assert, in one way or another, that the crucial part of Christian faith is what is lived out in real life, and that any instance of Christian faith must somehow be determinative of observable behavior, in concrete communities, which are formed by, focused around, particular practices.[12]

John Wesley would, I think, endorse some of this language of "practices." Wesley, sometimes portrayed as primarily an evangelist, was in fact equally gifted in organizing real, lived communities, and he always wanted to make sure that enduring life changes were occurring in the people who had responded to his preaching. He was not interested in merely providing a spiritual thrill or an ephemeral passion. In this basic sense, Wesley clearly was about promoting a practical faith.[13] He wanted people to "practice their faith."

There have been some recent discussions of practices, however, which seem to come close to embodying a misunderstanding of the Christian faith which is as old as the faith itself, and one that was a particularly important misunderstanding during Wesley's time. That is, seeing Christianity as primarily something that one *does*, and ignoring the subjective experience of *being* a Christian.

In this vein, Robert Wuthnow, in an article in *The Christian Century*, spoke of a practice-oriented spirituality, and contrasted this with a "seeker-oriented" spirituality of "indwelling."[14] Wuthnow applauded the former and denigrated the latter, making it seem as if any model for spirituality other than the life defined by practices would lead to emotional self-delusion and obsession with our own immediate needs.

I think Wesleyans will lose sight of a crucial part of the truth of our tradition, however, if, in the midst all of this present emphasis on the practice of the faith, we forget an important admonition from John Wesley. In a letter to "John Smith" in 1745 Wesley warned his reader that

> I would rather say faith is 'productive of all Christian *holiness*,' than 'of all Christian *practice*'; because men are so exceeding apt to rest in 'practice', so called, I mean in *outside religion*; whereas *true*

---

12. See especially Dorothy C. Bass's recent book, *Practicing Our Faith*.

13. See my "*Orthokardia*"; and Maddox, "John Wesley—Practical Theologian?"

14. Wuthnow, "Spiritual Practice."

religion is eminently seated in the heart, renewed in the image of
him that created us.[15] [emphasis his]

Looking seriously at the New Testament with all of its references to
the heart, to love, to joy, to peace, etc., one cannot help but think that a
"heart religion" is the minimum requirement for taking the Bible seriously.
But taking heart religion as our paradigm means that we have an ongoing,
twofold task of clarification. On one front, the battle will always be over
understanding the nature of these religious "affections" or "tempers" so
that they are not just seen as episodic, intense feelings, but as dispositions
for all of life, master passions which shape all behavior whether they are
consciously felt or not.

While guarding against this over-emphasis on the inner, felt experience, though, those who promote heart religion must also be wary on
another front as well, that which Wesley warns us about in his quote.
Emphasizing "practice" in an exclusive and single-minded way can lead
to a deadening moralism that will ignore the heart's yearning for holiness.
No matter how compelling and complete the practice appears to be, if it
is not done with the goal of either growing or expressing our gratitude for
salvation, our joy in being rightly-related to God, our love for God and
neighbor, it has not achieved its purpose. As Wesley said in his sermon
"The Way to the Kingdom":

> Yea, two persons may do the same outward work—suppose, feed-
> ing the hungry, or clothing the naked—and in the meantime one
> of these may be truly religious and the other have no religion at all;
> for the one may act from the love of God, and the other from the
> love of praise. So manifest is it that although true religion naturally
> leads to every good word and work, yet the real nature thereof lies
> deeper still, even in the 'hidden man of the heart.' (# 7, 220).

Of some help in seeing the potentially crucial difference between
an orientation of "practices" and an orientation of "heart holiness" is the
distinction that the philosopher Robert C. Roberts makes between virtues related to the will and motivational virtues. In his essay titled "Will
Power and the Virtues," Roberts says the motivational (or "substantive")
virtues have to do with what we desire. Examples would be compassion
or friendship. The will-power-related virtues, on the other hand, are pri-

15. *Works*, 2:179, letter of December 30, 1745.

marily "corrective" in that they are needed mainly when we experience conflicting desires. Examples would be courage or self-control.

Those who exemplify perfectly the motivational virtues in the Christian context would be those who fundamentally desire the love of God and neighbor. Such exemplars Roberts (and the church) call "saints." Those who have conflicting desires—who are not marked by the "purity of heart" of the saints—will need such corrective virtues as courage and self-control, and those who prevail in such inner struggles Roberts labels "heroes" rather than "saints." (Overcoming the character flaws which lead to conflicting desires is the classic plot of tragedy, and the protagonists of such stories, are often referred to as "heroes.")

Roberts asserts, and Wesleyan theologians would agree, that *both* kinds of virtue are required in the Christian life since even those most "pure in heart" are still in need of the will power virtues in this world of temptation. We need to be part saint and part hero, to use Roberts's language. This brings us back to the problem with a single-minded emphasis on "practices" as the defining feature of the Christian life.

We need to see that for Wesley the Christian life is not simply a collection of proper deeds to do, but also as entailing *a distinctive manner of doing them*. This means that being a Christian is not just a question of knowing what to do and then doing it, but it is also a question of *how* these deeds are done. "The Lord loves a cheerful giver," means that the Lord disapproves not only of those who don't give enough, but also of those who don't give cheerfully, no matter how much they throw in the plate. The gratitude of a cheerful giver comes from a heart touched by grace, from a life of holiness.

Surely we can say that a person who fails to perform certain obligatory Christian deeds is deficient of faith. But we also need to say that faith is more than the performance of such deeds: it also involves a certain *kind* of performance; a certain "spirit" in the way one performs them. Put differently, the key to authentic faith seems to lie not just in the verbs, but in the adverbs; not just in the nouns, but in the adjectives.[16] This can be hard to capture in "practice" language, which can invite an objectifying, de-personalizing view of the faith.

---

16. Thanks to Rick Steele for this particular way of phrasing things.

These remarks can be seen, of course, as nothing more than a kind of gloss on Paul's admonition in 1 Cor 13:3—"If I give all I possess to the poor and surrender my body to the flames, but have not love, I gain nothing" (NIV). And it was Jesus himself who said in the Sermon of the Mount that we must not hate, let alone murder, must not even lust, let alone commit adultery (Matt 5:21–29).

So while it is possible to get lost in an interior labyrinth, and lose contact with the God of the real, external world, by focusing solely on our inner experience, it is also possible to be so defined by one's outward and observable life that one neglects the interior life, the life of the heart. When that is the case, we risk becoming, as Wesley once put it, like "'whited sepulchres,' fair without and foul within."[17]

If we can avoid being cowed away from using the biblical heart language by this current intellectual trend of speaking primarily about "practices," and so avoid the dangers of emphasizing exclusively the visible side of the Christian life, then we can use Wesley's theology in truly "practical" ways.[18]

Wesley's Practical Theology

With these caveats concerning the "primacy of practice" in mind we can now return to the larger question of how one should understand practical theology in Wesleyan terms. Let us consider the remaining four criteria for practical theology as Maddox describes them—that a practical theology needs to not only emphasize the primacy of practices, but that it should be transformative, holistic, contextual and occasional. Of these, it is clear that most important for describing the truly practical nature of Wesley's theology are the "transformative" and "holistic" elements. The "contextual" and "occasional" elements on Maddox's model aptly describe Wesley's *mode* of doing theology—he did react to the events as they occurred, sometimes in letters, treatises or abridgements, rather than writ-

17. Wesley's comment on Luke 11:44 in his *N.T. Notes.*

18. A balanced emphasis on practices, which sees them—and the narratives which hold them in place—as working toward their proper end of holiness, the truly religious affections of the heart—can be found in Hauerwas, Murphy, and Nation, *Theology Without Foundations.* See especially Richard B. Steele's article on "Narrative Theology and the Religious Affections," 163–79.

ing one comprehensive, systematic tome covering all doctrines within one cover. But when describing his theology as "per se practical," what I see as truly essential is the *transformative* and *holistic* use of the affections of the heart as the necessarily constitutive elements of the Christian life.

That is why it made sense for Wesley to say that if one did not have the religious affections, one was not a mature Christian—if you don't love God and your neighbor, you have not really understood what it means to have your sins forgiven or to be graced with freedom—in short, you have not fully understood the gospel.

As John R. Tyson states in his article "Essential Doctrines and Real Religion: Theological Method in Wesley's Sermons on Several Occasions":

> For Wesley, theological 'essentials' were those producing 'real religion.' The truthfulness of a doctrine inhered not only in its veracity, but also its vitality . . . What seems most "essential" about Wesley's doctrines was his willingness to affirm classical Christian teaching in solid connection with the larger context of Christian living. He had a pervasive sense of the inner symmetry of Christian theology. His appreciation for the "analogy of faith" felt the wholeness within Christian teaching and sought to apply it in order to produce whole Christian lives. [19]

Webster's Ninth Collegiate Dictionary lists one meaning of "practical" as meaning "actively engaged in some course of action or occupation," and when Maddox emphasizes the contextual and occasional nature of Wesley's theologizing, this definition would fit. However, Webster's also says that practical can mean "capable of being put to use or account: useful." This, I think, is the primary reason why Wesley's theology is practical—it is directly useful in the process of formation, and this, in large part, because his theology is *expressed* in the *language* of formation—the language of the heart. That is why, as I stated in chapter 1, that the three "doctrines" of repentance, faith and holiness were the best summary of Christianity for Wesley. They are the most useful and, therefore, practical. [20]

19. Tyson, "Essential Doctrines," 175.

20. The problem with several contemporary works on doctrine in the Wesleyan tradition is that the specifically heart-related features of his theology that make his theology so practical are typically filtered out of the portrayal of Wesley's theological vision. See my critique of several of these in "Wesley's 'Main Doctrines.'"

Teaching Wesley's Practical Theology and its Relationship to the Essential Christian Doctrines

If, as I have asserted, the "renewal of the heart" is the orienting concern of Wesley's theology, legitimate questions arise about the role of the larger sweep of Christian doctrine in teaching Wesleyan practical theology. One way of putting this would be to ask: "In teaching and engendering the faith, should good Wesleyans relate to the essential Christian doctrines, such as the Trinity, the two natures of Christ, the sacraments, etc., any differently than Wesley related to these essential Christian doctrines?" My answer to this question is "no."[21]

Let me say more about what I mean by "essential Christian doctrines." In Wesley's time, this would refer to things like the broadly ecumenical doctrines found in the *Homilies*, the "Articles of Religion" and the *Book of Common Prayer* of the Church of England. For the contemporary United Methodist Church, I mean by essential doctrine what is specified in the *Book of Discipline*, that is, the *Standard Sermons* of Wesley, his *N.T. Notes*, and Wesley's abridged "Articles of Religion." In that context, I think we should not relate to these doctrines any differently than the way that Wesley did in his day.

In the Wesleyan tradition, it is undeniably important to have a coherent doctrinal framework *in the background* of the Christian life, which can be referred to as a kind of grammar of the Christian life.[22] But just as we do not typically learn a language—especially our first language—by studying its grammar first, so Christianity should not be initially taught by emphasizing the essential Christian doctrines—and here I am not talking only about catechism for young teenagers, but even, and *especially*, theology for seminarians, especially given their increasingly common need for adult remedial catechesis.[23] Basic Christian formation and theological

---

21. For more on this distinction, see my discussion of Ted Campbell's work, 6–7.

22. On seeing theology as grammar, see not only Paul Holmer's work, which makes use of a remark by Wittgenstein in *Grammar of Faith*, but also Wesley's Preface to his *Explanatory Notes Upon the New Testament*, where he speaks about divinity as the grammar of the Holy Ghost (9–10). "Divinity," for Wesley, would be the equivalent of what we might term "practical theology" or "spiritual formation writings."

23. See the reference to this need by Greg Jones, Dean of Duke Divinity School, in his essay "Beliefs, Desires, Practices and the Ends of Theological Education," in Volf and Bass, *Practicing Theology*, 185–205, esp. 186ff.

education should, on Wesley's understanding, be concerned with shaping that metaphorical center of the human called the "heart." Unfortunately, this is not, in the first instance, done through the abstraction-centered paradigm that much higher education—including much theological education—values so highly, the kind abstract approach in evidence in the typical theology textbooks in use today.

Neither is this necessarily accomplished, as some seminaries seem to think, simply by adding a required course or two in spiritual formation, or putting everyone into a covenant discipleship group, though those are positive steps. To be true to Wesley's vision of Christianity, perhaps we should invite people—*in our theology courses*—to reflect not, in the first place about epistemology, the Trinity, or even the saving work of the cross of Christ, but on a series of questions—questions about their own lives. These questions might include:

> Who or what do you now love? What is it that you now take joy in? What is it that brings you peace? Are you happy now? Why or why not? What makes you afraid? What makes you angry? What makes you impatient? What kind of actions are you performing in the name of love? How is your life an expression of the joy of your salvation? What kind of behaviors in your life should be ruled-out if you have the peace that passes understanding?

When we have their answers to those questions, we will then be able to tell our students how the gospel proposes its own, distinctive answers to these questions as we outline the contours of the Christian life. Then we can start helping our students making the transition to that vision of a renewed heart, and we will not be doing it through a pedagogy of abstraction, but instead through a pedagogy of concrete imitation that can delight and enliven, rather than bore and alienate as theology classes all-too-often do.

Asking "heart" questions can make clear what the shape or grammar of their hearts now looks like, but it can also open up the possibility of adopting an alternative grammar—the grammar of a heart shaped by the gospel as conveyed in the basic doctrines of the faith. This alternative grammar is one that they can then hold onto, and live into, as a model for imitation. In *that* context, then, the traditional doctrines, the essential Christian doctrines—could be meaningfully taught.

The Inseparability of Theology and Spiritual Formation

Theologians, then, should be about describing what should be, for the Christian, the ultimate objects of our love and joy and why, what we should fear and why, etc., as well as what behaviors these affections should dispose us. But one of the best ways to promote this is having our "coherent doctrinal framework" that lies in the background of these questions itself be couched and expressed in the language of the heart. When we *begin* our theological ventures with consideration of doctrines like the Trinity or the nature of the salvation brought by the cross, we invite a different mindset and approach—what people in higher education (often condescendingly and self-servingly) like to call a "critical thinking" perspective. Here, doubt is privileged and faith and trust are seen with great suspicion. Once this method begins it sometimes never ends, with an ever-deepening gyre of confusions about proper epistemic warrants and foundations, meaning and reference, truth and validity.

On this point, Ellen Charry's analogy between theology and medicine is very apt. Charry says that the kind of knowledge that John Locke's epistemic pronouncements would allow, the standard that has so hamstrung theology in the last two hundred years—a knowledge separated from trust—was never the kind of knowledge that most of the Christian theologians of the tradition were looking for anyway. This means that trying to attain such knowledge is time spent distracted from our real goal. Accordingly, theology's failure to meet this standard should not be too bothersome to Christians, for while theology cannot meet this standard, neither can, as Charry points out, medicine, and yet we use medicine all of the time. This comparison to medicine can make clear just how theology per se (and not just some sub-field of it) can be "practical." On this model, we should relate to abstract, doctrinal theology in the same way that Wesley did: only as necessary to make clear the nature of, and clear up problems in, the Christian way of life.

Dr. Susan Felch, professor of English at Calvin College, has said that in her field of interpreting literature, the practitioners often align "complexity" with "perplexity" and assume that both necessarily entail critical distance, disbelief and doubt. As opposed to this paradigm, Felch offers another pedagogical approach emphasizing critical *imitation that leads to discovery*, and I think that is what we should be about as people who teach Christian theology.[24]

What would this mean in specific terms? Perhaps it would mean following Wesley's biographical emphasis in his *Arminian Magazine* and devoting significant parts of our theology classes to helping our students see the renewed hearts in some of the saints who have gone before us— seeing how their loves and fears, hopes and angers were re-arranged and re-ordered by the gospel, and how these affections were lived-out in real life—and *only then* trying to understand the logic or the grammar of this gospel that renews hearts.

This is one of the absolutely essential features of Wesley's thought— Christian truth had to be expressed in livable and imitable ways. This is why William Abraham has missed the genius of Wesley's theological vision when he denigrates Wesley's "heart" and "affection" language. This attitude is reflected in Abraham's *The Logic of Evangelism* where he says that the emphasis of Wesley (and Jonathan Edwards) on religious affections and the "response of the individual" has been the "undoing of modern evangelism."[25] In his more recent *Canon and Criterion in Christian Theology*, Abraham complains that while Wesley was "resolutely committed to the doctrine of the Trinity, it has been displaced by his doctrine of the Christian life in the analogy of faith."[26]

Wesley offers *not* a foundationalism of the Christian life, as Abraham seems to imply, because the affections cannot be generated or sustained outside of our relationship to the triune God made known to us through the life, teachings, death and resurrection of Jesus Christ. When we take the life of the heart seriously we can see how the gospel-shaped heart is not self-sufficient or complete in itself, but only exists as it stands rightly-related to the one true God. I have great sympathy with Abrahams's concern to avoid "doctrinal amnesia,"[27] but I am equally concerned with not

24. From her unpublished paper "You Cannot Teach a Child Disbelief" delivered at Pepperdine University's conference on Christian vocation, October 2002.

25. Abraham, *Logic of Evangelism*, 58–59.

26. Abraham, *Canon and Criterion*, 216 n. 1. In his address to the Wesleyan Theological Society, subsequently published as "The End of Wesleyan Theology," Abraham acknowledges that his reading and mine of Wesley on the affections are the two basic options currently debated. See page 14.

27. See Abraham, *Waking from Doctrinal Amnesia*.

distorting Wesley's vision of Christianity by teaching and using doctrine in ways that work against embodying Christianity as the renewal of the heart. Abraham has failed to see that by putting Christianity in terms of the life of the heart, Wesley has made a very accessible, and (crucially important) *imitable*, depiction of what it means to be a Christian.

This act of imitation does not entail a turn of one's eyes to *one's own* experience, or even necessarily the *experience of another*. The kind of imitation I am talking about involves turning one's eyes to see *the reality that is forming* the experience of the one we are imitating. At the beginning of the process we might catch a vision of a holy life being lived out by an exemplar—either a contemporary person, or a historical figure described in the literature of the tradition. We find it immensely attractive, and so we pay close attention to this life. But in the end, the process of formation comes about not by looking *at* the exemplar, by looking *with* the exemplar.

Another way of teaching Wesley's views on the essential doctrines might be to begin by studying some of the classic liturgies of the tradition and ask what kind of life they are trying to form. One could then work backwards from their vision of the Christian life to the doctrinal truths that are expressed in these liturgies. One of the implications of this Wesleyan vision of what is essential to Christianity is that Christianity is first and last a form of life, not merely a form of thought, and Don Saliers's work on worship and theology is very suggestive for the role of liturgy in primary theological orientation. Worship not only reflects a form of life, worship itself can be seen as a form of life.[28]

This means that both teaching Christian doctrine and leading people in a program of spiritual formation entail attempting what Kierkegaard called an "existence communication." Instead of seeing theology and spiritual formation as related to each other as dialectic is related to rhetoric in the medieval *trivium*—where dialectic establishes the "truth" and rhetoric merely is about communicating the truth convincingly—we need to re-envision both disciplines, especially in the Wesleyan tradition, as ultimately inseparable and symbiotically related.[29]

28. Saliers, *Worship as Theology*.

29. To see the irony of disconnecting theology from life, see Kierkegaard's *Journal* on "The Professor":

Wesley said in his "Earnest Appeal" that what he wanted to do is make people "virtuous and happy, easy in themselves and useful to others,"[30] and if our theological reflections begin with that vision, then perhaps the guild of theologians will get fewer complaints that what we put out "won't preach"—a criticism to be taken seriously in the Wesleyan tradition. The life of love and joy and peace in Christ is what we have to offer to the world. Wesleyans have the conviction that this is inherently attractive. The Christian should approach our under-catechized members—and non-Christians as well—with the awareness that we are the salt of the earth, and if we cannot season their lives, then we have nothing to offer.[31] This is not a foundationalism of the lived life—the foundation of this life is the Trinity as worshipped in hymn, sermon and Eucharist.

Stanley Grenz has asserted that evangelicalism is best understood in terms of spirituality and only secondarily as a set of doctrinal distinctives.[32] Especially if "evangelicals" see themselves as in the tradition of Wesley, such an evaluation would be a positive reflection of their fidelity to this tradition. Those who emphasize spirituality—the shape and form of one's life—know what the "doctrinal distinctives" are for, and they put them where they belong—enfleshed in the lived Christian life.[33]

> Let us take mathematics. It is very possible that a celebrated mathematician, e.g., might become a martyr to his science—hence there is nothing to hinder me from becoming a professor of the subject he lectured upon, for here the essential thing is a doctrine, science, and the personal life of the teacher is accidental.
>
> But ethico-religiously, and Christianly in particular, there is no doctrine that can be regarded as essential while the personal life of the teacher is accidental: here the essential thing is imitation. What nonsense then that one, instead of following Christ and the Apostles, and suffering what they suffered—that one instead should become a professor. Of what?—Why, that Christ was crucified and the Apostles scourged.
>
> Nothing was lacking but that on Golgotha there had been a professor present who promptly installed himself as professor . . . of theology? It is true, we know, that at that time theology had not yet emerged, so at that time it would have been clear that, if he would become professor of anything, it must have been of the fact that Christ was crucified—to become professor of . . . that somebody else was put to death.

From Walter Lowrie's biography *Kierkegaard*, 507.

30. *Works*, vol. 11, "An Earnest Appeal to Men of Reason and Religion," 51.

31. S. T. Kimbrough once remarked that this was the evangelistic approach of the Christian minority in Nepal.

32. Grenz, *Revisioning Evangelical Theology*, 58.

33. On this point I think it is helpful to note what two influential biblical scholars, who happen to be in the Wesleyan tradition, have said about the authority of the Bible.

Recent philosophers, like John Cottingham, Mark Wynn, and William Wainwright have, independent of any concern for Wesley, made the case that in order for the truth of religion to be understood and assented to, the heart must first be properly disposed. Wainwright makes the telling comparison with the smoker who wants to quit: it is not more information about how bad smoking is that the smoker needs. The smoker needs his desires re-ordered so that the force of the arguments against smoking can be appreciated. Related to this approach is the expanding field of virtue epistemology, whose proponents say that to know the truth, one must first develop certain virtues. If you are not marked by empathy, humility and honesty, there are truths you will never know. When the heart changes, new truths are available.[34]

Based on what I have emphasized from the beginning of this present work, then, there are three reasons why those influenced by Wesley ought not to translate or filter out Wesley's language of life experience—the language of the heart and its affections—when we describe what is essential to Christianity in various theological contexts:

1) Doing so would evacuate Wesley's theology of not only its particular style, but also much of its essential content;

2) Contemporary thinkers are finally coming to terms with what important and complex realities "affections" truly are, allowing us to understand them in the full-orbed way they have been seen by most of the Christian tradition, going back to Aquinas and Augustine and the Scripture itself; and

3) This heart language itself is the most important reason why Wesley's theology is a truly practical theology. Speaking of doctrines in terms of life experiences is necessary if our practical

Joel Green, in his article "Contribute or Capitulate?" says, ". . . the authority of scripture is best discerned in the lives (and not only the assertions) of those communities oriented around Scripture . . ." (81–82). Similarly, Richard Hays, referring to a passage in Paul's writings says that Paul is there working out "the claim that the true meaning of Scripture is made manifest in the transformed lives of the community of faith" (Hays, *Echoes of Scripture in the Letters of Paul*, xiii).

34. See Wainwright's *Reason and the Heart*; Cottingham's *Spiritual Dimension*; Wynn's *Emotional Experience and Religious Understanding*, and Roberts and Wood, *Intellectual Virtues*.

theological task is to be the same as Wesley's—that is, to describe the Christian character, promise it can be ours, and describe how to attain it.

Madame Bovary in Flaubert's famous novel of that name made a wreck of her life because she tried to discover just what was meant, in life, by the words "joy," "passion," "intoxication"—words that had seemed so beautiful to her in books.[35] I think that many people today—Christian and otherwise—are making a wreck of their lives in the fashion of Madame Bovary—relying on the images of joy and passion that our often-toxic culture floats out into the world. Wesley's vision of Christianity—and his theology in the key of the affections—offers a vision where such issues are not seen as irrelevant, or are subordinated to some sort of second-ary, "application" field of pastoral theology, but are the central substance addressed in foundational theological discourse. Questions about the nature of true joy, love and peace are taken with the utmost seriousness, and the Scriptures, as interpreted by reason and tradition, are enlisted to help shape and create such experiences—experiences that don't lead to a ruined life a la Bovary, but, to use Wesley's famous couplet, to all "happi-ness and holiness."[36]

If this paradigm is a workable one, if it is possible to live, and spread, Wesley's vision of Christianity today with integrity, then it is fair to ask for a few specific ways that this understanding of heart religion might be conveyed beyond the classroom, in the real world, and in a truly practical way. That is the task to which I turn to in the final chapter.

---

35. Flaubert, *Madame Bovary*, 34. The book was first published in Paris in 1857.

36. Lest the reader become concerned about this approach losing sight of larger theological issue of the *truth* of our doctrines, I would make clear that seeing doctrine as primarily serving the purpose of bringing about the renewal of the heart does not give up any claims to the realism and reference of our doctrines. Cf. Charry's *By the Renewal of Your Minds*, 30–31, n. 4 where she sees no contradiction between holding both a realistic referential view of doctrine and also emphasizing doctrine's instrumental dimension.

7   Renewing the Heart through Preaching, Counseling, and Evangelism

Practical Theology, the Heart, and Narrative

If this way of thinking about Christianity called a "Wesleyan heart religion" can actually be a viable paradigm for Christian living today one might fairly ask for some concrete advice on how to translate Wesley's "affection" talk into meaningful discourse today. Perhaps we could just settle for talk of a Christian vision of life that is "holistic"[1] (or "wholistic"), hoping that the full complexities of the heart as Wesley understood it might somehow come through this way. I think, however, that most would agree that these terms are just too vague to be helpful. Saying, in effect, his theology "covers it all" does not even begin to tell of what the "all" might consist.

Neither, I think, is a program of trying to revivify the classical language of the "affections" as being inescapably cognitive likely to be effective, at least in the short run. I think the "adversary" view of the emotions (to which Nussbaum referred—see chapter 3) is too firmly entrenched in our present culture to lead to anything but confusion if we started emphasizing a "theology of the affections" or some such program.

Should we then just despair of the whole project? No, but not simply because we would be leaving Wesley behind. We cannot despair of the project of heart religion because that would leave the gospel behind. We must promote Christianity through the use of the first order language of the heart, and not be daunted by fear of constantly falling into misinterpretation, because the gospel itself trusts the power of the words "faith,"

---

1. This is common terminology in spiritual formation circles to imply that everything in our lives should be touched by the gospel. This has lately been a tendency in Randy Maddox's writing about Wesley as well. See his "'Celebrating the Whole Wesley,'" as well as Paul Chilcote's *Recapturing The Wesley's Vision*.

"love," "joy," and "peace." If we cannot trust them then, in the end, we cannot trust the gospel.

Yes, there will *always* be possible misinterpretations of this heart language, but that is part of what it means to try to assert *any* truth in a world where we live as finite, fallible, sinful and broken people. Christians in the Wesleyan tradition, though, cannot let that hamstring them from their calling—to spread holiness, the renewal of the heart. If and when misunderstandings arise, we simply must address them, given the tools at hand that we have. In this book, I have tried to show that between Wesley's vision of heart religion and some recent, sophisticated under-standings of emotion, all guided by the Holy Spirit, we have all that we need for this gospel calling.

Consistent with how Wesley saw sanctification or holiness growing and spreading, we need to have confidence in the Holy Spirit's ability to use our own lives to give meaning to our words. If we speak of "love" and our hearers see the reality of that term in the shape of our whole lives, then the gospel will be spread. The meaning of the "works of the flesh" will become obvious when they start disappearing from our lives, and the "fruit of the Spirit" will be understood by others when these fruit start growing in us.

In chapter 3 we noted that our contemporary theorists of emotion all saw an important link between the affections and narrative, and this link is important in seeing how we can propagate Wesley's vision of heart religion today. Below, as a way of expressing Wesley's vision, I will give several narrative-related examples of how the affections of the heart can be made flesh by the church today. To authorize this use of narrative in a practical theology that aims at promoting *orthokardia*, let me quote Nussbaum on the link between emotions and narrative:

> . . . if emotions are as Proust describes them, they have a compli-
> cated cognitive structure that is in part narrative in form, involving
> a story of our relation to cherished objects that extends over time.
> Ultimately, we cannot understand the Baron's love, for example,
> without knowing a great deal about the history of patterns of at-
> tachment that extend back into his childhood. Past loves shadow
> present attachments, and take up residence within them. This, in
> turn, suggests that in order to talk well about them we will need to
> turn to texts that contain a narrative dimension, thus deepening
> and refining our grasp of ourselves as beings with a complicated

temporal history. . . . If we accept his view of what the emotions are, we should agree, to the extent of making a place for literature (and other works of art) within moral philosophy, alongside more conventional philosophical texts. Once again: an account of human reasoning based only upon abstract texts such as are conventional in moral philosophy is likely to prove too simple to offer us the type of self understanding we need.[2]

On this point, we should be reminded of Wesley's own writing practices which included diaries, published journals, letters and sermons which, to different degrees, all have a narrative cast to them, not to mention, of course, his explicit reliance on biographical sketches of Methodist saints as portrayed in *The Arminian Magazine*. Since the affections or emotions are creatures of time, these different narrative forms which reflect time in different ways are not incidental to Wesley's theological project, but are essential to it. Below I will use several examples of different kinds of narratives, including some from my own life, as well as examples from that type of narrative that is most accessible to people today, the narrative films of the popular cinema. In many popular films we see reflections of our culture's deep yearning for the renewal of the heart.

In offering these narratives for consideration, I hope we can also see how Wesley's vision of heart religion can find practical expression in a variety of constitutive Christian activities, including preaching, counseling and evangelism. I do not offer these reflections in the hopes of laying down some necessary and determinative paradigm for these activities. I offer them simply as ways to show that some specific and necessary acts of Christian spiritual formation are especially empowered by the vision of Christianity that guided Wesley—the religion of the heart.

The Renewal of the Human Heart as a Theme in Artistic Narrative Expression

Conversion, preaching, pastoral counseling, leading worship, and other actions that are a part of "spiritual formation" are all concerned, in one way or another, with human change. Passion for human change, though, is hardly restricted to those who occupy themselves with specifically

2. Nussbaum, *Upheavals*, 2–3.

religious concerns. This theme is powerfully expressed in many artistic productions of recent Western culture.

One recent cinematic example of the drama of human change can be seen in *Ground Hog Day*. In this film, Bill Murray is trapped repeating a particular February 2nd—Ground Hog Day. No matter what he does, when he wakes the next morning it is still Ground Hog Day. He is seemingly trapped on an endless wheel of "rebirth" where the cycles of history cannot be changed. Finally, after trying everything to make a difference—including self-indulgent pleasure seeking and even suicide—his character arrives at a point of change. He decides to start doing what he can to improve the world rather than use and exploit the world for his own desires. When his efforts for improvement lead him to live one complete day of selfless service to others, he ends up winning the love of the woman whom he previously simply sought to seduce, and he awakens literally to a brand new day. Ground Hog Day is over. He has new life.

Another story with human change at its center is Charles Dickens's *A Christmas Carol*. We see Scrooge with his odious, contemptible self-concern, totally curved in on himself, and the reader (or viewer) rightly recoils. Through his fateful encounter with three different apparitions, however, Scrooge undergoes a transformation from miserly self-concern to charity and compassion. Our reaction to Scrooge changes accordingly, from being repelled from him to having sympathy towards him, and even having vicarious joy over his new life, leading to a hope that such transformations can take place in others, or perhaps, even in ourselves.

Other cinematic examples of this theme would include *Babette's Feast* (where an elaborate feast takes on eucharistic qualities and transforms the lives of self-centered and judgmental church goers) and, of course, the classic *It's A Wonderful Life*, where Jimmy Stewart's character, George Bailey, goes from the brink of suicide to embracing life, even if it includes punishment and disgrace, because he has received new eyes to see and new ears to hear. *About a Boy* would be a more recent example of power and attraction of the transformative change from egocentrism to concern for others.

The drama of human change can also be found at the heart of the movie *Forrest Gump*, a film that has peculiar relevance to the concerns of a Wesleyan heart religion. In this film we see the saga not so much of the dynamics of *transformation* operating in Gump's own life, but instead the dynamics of *steadfastness*, *adherence* and *faithfulness* in the face of a world that invites corrupting change and vicious formation. As Gump's girlfriend, Jenny, undergoes all the culturally-invited transformations of three decades in the twentieth century, Gump remains fixed.

The question which Forrest Gump poses in the penultimate scene of the movie captures this tension, and in some ways it is a question which lies behind the concerns about heart religion. Gump asks, "Is it Lieutenant Dan or Mama who's right?" In other words, do we have a fixed destiny, or are we just floating on the apparently random breezes of the exigencies of life? The question is expressed symbolically as well in the film by a feather, which floats apparently haphazardly—but lands strategically—at both the beginning and end of the movie. Are we free or determined? The possibilities for human change, and the course of human conduct, are greatly affected by the answer we give to that question.

When we are working within a Wesleyan theological paradigm, the answer we must give is as complex and true to life as the movement of the feather in the film. That is to say, conjunctions of human freedom and God's grace do occur, even if at times these transformative conjunctions seem entirely serendipitous. Life has undeniably brutal and wounding aspects, many of which seem to result from the misuse of human freedom (for example, the incest Jenny suffered at the hands of her father). But just as undeniably, transforming grace visits us in the midst of our brokenness (as Forrest's friendship is a recurrent note of grace in Jenny's life).

Finally, as Wesleyan Christians, our answer to Gump's musings about freedom and determinism must be Gump's own answer: "I think it's both." Human sin can leave us, at times, with only a very limited set of options with which to exercise our human freedom, but God's grace can inhabit even the most limited options to make possible the flourishing of human life. As we will see, this dynamic of grace-in-freedom often comes to a point in our answers to the questions: "What shall be the *object* of your heart's attention?" and "To what form of life is your heart *disposing* you?" This can be seen in one of the most popular musicals of the American stage and screen, *The Music Man*.

An Example of Transformation in Community: *The Music Man*[3]

In *The Music Man*, we see a town transformed by a charismatic man. His vision of a boy's band enlivens the small Iowa town of "River City" and puts a spring in the step of all those caught up in the vision. On first viewing, one might say that this film is a sarcastic mocking of the Christian vision of life. The protagonist, Harold Hill, with the gestures and inflections of a revivalist preacher, spends most of the play trying to sell the town instruments and uniforms for a boy's band that he has no intention of actually creating. Here we could see dramatized a Marxist critique of Christianity which sees the church as mainly interested in the continuing financial support by the rank and file membership by spouting delusional stories of "pie in the sky, by and by." Some post-modernists would have Christianity portrayed primarily in terms of its economic and power relationships, and on this view Harold Hill could be seen as a symbol of the desire to control and manipulate everything for the bottom line of power and material gain.

The Music Man, however, provides a subtler analysis of the possibilities of human transformation in the context of community that goes beyond such caricatures, for it is the changes that take place *in spite of* his desire to manipulate and control that are most compelling. In the end, Harold Hill encounters the self-sacrificial love of Marian who is willing to acknowledge his deceptive intentions but loves him nonetheless. The reason for this, in part at least, is the excitement that Hill's vision of the boy's band has brought about in Marian's own little brother.

Harold Hill "got his foot caught in the door" by seeing genuine love shown towards him, a love that knows who he truly is, yet seeks his best interest in spite of that knowledge. Even more amazingly, Harold Hill is caught up in his own (what he presumed to be totally fictive) vision of a boy's band. In the end, while handcuffed by the local police, he begins to

---

3. Parts of what follows originally appeared in Chilcote, *Wesleyan Tradition*, 118–22. I have chosen *The Music Man* even though it is almost fifty years old, for two reasons. First, it is regarded as one of the classics of musical theater, often staged in high schools and community theaters and is currently being brought back in a revival on Broadway. (I have been surprised at the number of college students who are familiar with it because of high school productions.) Secondly, the film version is available on video and DVD should anyone want to study on their own how this play illustrates these dynamics.

conduct the band and, though halting, uncertain and far from perfect, the band begins to play recognizable music.

Acts of faith and unconditional agape love do in fact bring about real transformation but it is only when *all* of reality is acknowledged. Marian held up to Harold both a well polished mirror *but also* a vision of a new and different way of life. So it is with the church. When we are called to tell the truth to one another, we must remember *both* the true reality of our individual and corporate lives as they are now, *but also* the transforming good news of forgiveness, hope, and love which our tradition has handed on to us.

At the end of the *Music Man* this dual focus is beautifully portrayed as we see two people transformed because of their interaction with each other. From the beginning of the play, the theme music for Marian "the librarian" (the guardian of the community's higher values, literally and figuratively, in her role as librarian) has been "Goodnight My Someone." This song is all about a longing for an indeterminate object for romantic love, a longing that is unfulfilled. (Her mother says her longing was un-fulfilled because Marian's vision of the love object was a combination of "St. Patrick, Paul Bunyan, and Noah Webster," in other words, that she had over-idealized the object for human love.)

Harold Hill, the sham "professor," is, on the other hand, portrayed throughout the film with the theme song "Seventy-six Trombones" play-ing in the background. The booming bluster of the charismatic salesman blasting through to close the deal with all the subtlety of seventy-six trombones is a fittingly symbolic way of characterizing his attempts at worldly manipulation. In the final scenes of the film, however, we see the possibility of community shaping the heart reflected in the surprising swapping of these theme songs.

Harold has caught a vision of a life quite different from that which his life of high-pressure salesmanship has fostered, dominated as it was by manipulation and selfishness. This new vision is of a gentle, non-ma-nipulative love, exemplified in the witness of Marian's sacrifices for him. In an opposite way, Marian has decided to leave the realm of impossible ideals and decided to love a broken, and sinful man, but a man through whom good things come. Through the dramatic medium of a duet be-tween Harold and Marian, we see the evidence of this mutual transforma-tion. With each in separate rooms of a house where they are preparing for a romantic encounter, Harold begins singing Marian's theme song, "Goodnight My Someone," while Marian begins singing Harold's theme song, "Seventy-six Trombones."

Marian has started to accommodate into her abstract and idealistic dreamy view of love some of the bold brassiness of human reality (and more than a hint of sexuality, with her agreeing, finally, to meet the professor at the "foot bridge," the neighborhood romantic rendezvous spot.) On the other hand, Harold has stopped thinking only about himself and starts to fix his heart on a new vision—Marian's self-denying and self-giving love. By being real, one to another, and speaking frankly of the truths they know, while also being open to growing and transforming in areas they had not seriously considered before, Harold Hill and Marian, the librarian, offer imperfect, yet powerful, images of how Christians can grow together in community, each offering the other help in realizing their common goal of being fully alive.

Balancing the Multiple Objects of our Heart: A Pastoral Illustration

If we are to emphasize *both* being formed in the truths of the tradition *and* listening to the truths of our present reality and our contemporary community, we need to be attentive to the challenge of keeping these elements in balance. Like Marian and Harold, we have to pay attention to both the reality of who we are *and* the reality we are called to be. In other words, we must avoid fixing our hearts *only* the realities of life as we currently experience it, but neither can we focus solely on the truths of the tradition that paint our goal for us. The problem of holding these two realities in creative tension can be seen in some of the struggles in the contemporary church over social issues.

As a senior pastor of a church of just under 1,000 members in Waverly, Iowa, I was asked by several leaders in the congregation if we might have a series of presentations and discussion times on a variety of social issues during our Lenten Wednesday night suppers. After some discussion and much prayer, I agreed, but only if they would be structured in a certain way. This structure was not designed to lead to a particular consensus on any particular view of any particular social issue, it had to do with this tension between the truths of the tradition and the truths of our contemporary reality. While one week we would discuss abortion, and the next week homosexuality and on through a litany of the typical issues that are discussed today, there was to be a common pattern to our gatherings. At the end of that Lenten season, there were no mass defections from the church, or angry splits in the congregation, even though all of these divisive issues had in fact been talked about. I cannot claim absolute knowledge as to why the congregation came through that minefield unscathed, but it is my faith that the pattern in which these discussions were undertaken had something to do with it.

At the beginning of each week's deliberations I asked all to stand and sing *The Church's One Foundation Is Jesus Christ Her Lord*. We then discussed the issue of the week, often with representative so both "sides" speaking, and then, at the end of the session, we again stood and sang *The Church's One Foundation Is Jesus Christ Her Lord*. This embodied the truth that the basis for our community is not complete agreement on a whole laundry list of issues that the culture of this moment in history has presented to us. The basis for our community is Jesus Christ. We worship the God whom Jesus revealed and embodied, we receive the forgiveness of sins that his death on the cross purchased for us, and we are called to a new life in the Holy Spirit which came into the world in a special way after the resurrection of Jesus.

If I had refused to discuss these social issues and confined our Lenten topics only to creedal explications or the re-telling of biblical stories, the living tension where formation happens would have died. Likewise, if we had had the discussions of contemporary issues without singing, as a congregation, the hymn, (and thereby invoking all that the hymn proclaims), the tension between tradition's truths and the community's realities would also have died. Knowing where, when and how to fix the eyes of our heart is the necessary spiritual requirement for meaningfully addressing the potentially divisive issues that confront us today.

Preaching, Counseling, and Evangelism for the Renewal of the Heart

Having now seen the deep longing for heart renewal that can be found in our culture, and having seen a few examples of how the grammar of the heart can be invoked to understand and pattern that change, I want to shift my analysis to consider a few specifically Christian endeavors aimed at fostering heart change. Specifically, I want to consider three of the ways that the vocation of human change can be fostered by the work of the church. These are preaching, counseling and evangelism.

Though these are all functions typically assigned to the ordained pastor, the Wesleyan tradition of lay preaching, lay classes and bands for spiritual growth, and lay evangelism means that there is nothing especially clerical about these opportunities for heart renewal. Noting this does not diminish the necessarily sacramental nature of Wesley's model for spiritual growth, but it simply emphasizes that formation is not something primarily for the "professional" to do. *All* Christians are called to active participation in the vocation of embodying the fruit of the Spirit.[4]

Preaching Wesley's "House of Religion" by "Offering them Christ"

On Wesley's analysis, to help people grow in heart religion, we have to help them target their affections on the right objects. To understand how this "targeting" can work, let us look again at the three essential doctrines that John Wesley named as describing the doctrinal kernel of Christianity. By way of a reminder, this is how he summarized these three essential doctrines in his "Principles of a Methodist Farther Explained:"

> Our main doctrines, which include all the rest, are three—that of repentance, of faith, and of holiness. The first of these we account, as it were, the porch of religion; the next, the door; the third, religion itself.[5]

Now let us consider how we might preach so as to invite the congregation into living the truth of each of these essential doctrines by "offering them Christ" as the object of their hearts.

---

4. For an in-depth analysis of the role of sacraments in Wesley's theology, see Knight, *Presence of God in the Christian Life.*

5. *Works*, 9:227.

Preaching the "Porch of Repentance"

If we want to bring our hearers onto the "porch" of repentance of this "house" of Christianity, we must start by remembering the logic of how emotions/affections work. When we recall that emotions must take an object, we will understand very quickly that we should not point the people to their own sinfulness if we want them truly to repent. Targeting one's own sinfulness can only lead to one's feeling of guilt. Perhaps there are times when this is important in a particularly unawakened person, but more often than not, what is needed is to focus the attention of the hearer on that object which can best bring about an awareness of one's own sin. The Bible shows us that very often that best way to do this is to focus people not on their own sin, but on the holiness of God.

As we can see in both the Old and the New Testaments, we are often most vividly aware of our sinfulness not when someone comes along and wags a finger at us and tells us how bad we are, but when we catch a glimpse of God's holiness. In Isaiah's call to ministry (6:1ff), he is aware of the holiness of God, and the angels put this awareness into words, saying "holy, holy, holy." The first words out of Isaiah's mouth, however, are "Woe is me! I am lost. . . ." By seeing what true holiness is like, Isaiah becomes aware of just how unholy he is, just how far he is from the Image of God he was created to bear.

Similarly, in Luke 5, when Peter witnesses the miracle of the net full of fish, he shouts out to Jesus "Go away from me, Lord, for I am a sinful man." Jesus does not have to judge Peter or rub his nose in his sins to invite Peter onto the porch of repentance. He merely had to show God's holiness through the miracle of the net full of fish. When Peter was given this vision, all he could think of is fleeing, for he had became aware of his own sinfulness through an encounter with the Holy One.

As preachers, if we want to bring about repentance, we need to offer our people Christ. Let them behold the holiness of God revealed in Christ, the holiness of the uncompromising teacher of the Sermon on the Mount,[6] the holiness of the one who loved us so much that he gave his life for us, the holiness of the one who forgives his tormentors as he

---

6. Wesley, in his sermon "Original, Nature, Properties and Use of the Law" (*Works*, 2:34), said that one of the most important characteristics of the law is that it is holy (10ff).

writhes in pain on the cross. When people can catch a vision of such a Christ, perhaps through the word pictures that the preacher is called to paint, or perhaps through the words of the liturgy (and hopefully aided by the surrounding architecture and liturgical appointments), then they will be invited to consider the source of all holiness, and thus allow the Holy Spirit to lead them to true repentance and holiness.

Heart religion will become sentimental and romantic if one focuses on those aspects of reality which are themselves emotions. For instance, if the preacher spends a lot of time talking about how moving it is to behold the crucifixion of Christ, and talks about people being moved to tears by such a vision, he has strayed from offering them Christ himself and has gone to talk about the epi-phenomena that arise from beholding Christ—feelings. We cannot engender heart religion by targeting feelings, but only by targeting our attention on the objects which can generate renewed heart—God and the things of God.

Preaching the "Door of Faith"

If we want our hearers to walk through the door of faith as Wesley understood it, then we must speak of both fundamental meanings of "faith." We must invite the parishioners to grow both faith in the sense of the essential truths about who God is—that part of Christianity which can be put down on paper—but also, and even more importantly, faith as a disposition of one's heart—a personal trust in the truth of the gospel. To do this, we preachers have to present the object of Christian trust to the hearers.

While a big part of this is telling the "old, old story of Jesus and his love," describing the object of our faith can also take place not so much by describing the object directly, but by describing scenes where people are targeting God with their faith. In this sense, one could pay attention to the believers not in order to look *at* them, but to look *with* them, to gaze upon the objects that have given them the faith to go on.

One reason why preachers often refer to novels (or more often these days, TV programs or movies) as ways of illustrating their points is that the characters in these fictions are portrayed in a way that allows us to see where their hearts are fixed. Often in such artistic works we can see the object of people's hearts more readily than we can in real life. For instance, in *It's a Wonderful Life*, the people in Bedford Falls caught, over a period of many years, a glimpse of reality through the eyes of Jimmy Stewart's character's eyes and were inspired by his life of trusting faith to live a "wonderful life." They not only looked *at* George Bailey, they looked *with* him, and as we watched this whole process, we were invited to see reality through his eyes as well.

The goal of such fictional references, then, is to get people to see that it really is a wonderful life—and that God is a God who can be trusted—by attending to reality the way that Jimmy Stewart's character attended to it.[7] If, by offering them such references, our parishioners can see reality with discerning "eyes to see and ears to hear" as George Bailey saw it, then in a very real sense we are "offering Christ," even if the proximate object of our attention is George Bailey and not Christ himself.

Preaching the "House Itself"

This same pattern of offering Christ can be seen in the third part of Wesley's image of the house of Christianity, namely the house of holiness. Wesley understood holiness to be nothing but love.[8] We need not look very far in Scripture before the biblical understanding of love becomes clear, and that this love—*agape*—is not mere erotic or romantic love, nor is it the friendship of affinity groups.[9]

For vivid depictions of agape we, like Wesley, turn to Scripture. While many are familiar with 1 Corinthians 13 and its famous description of love that is read at most weddings, fewer will remember that there is an even more concise definition of love to be found in the New Testament. That is in 1 John 3:16, which reads: "We know love by this, that he laid down his life for us—and we ought to lay down our lives for one another" (NRSV). Our hearers can understand this self-sacrificial love that we are called to live out when we can point them to examples of it. When we look

---

7. Note well, here, that his was not a Pollyanna view of life—he was filled with greatest joy at the end of the film even while gladly embracing the prospect of worldly disgrace and prison!

8. See my book *As If the Heart Mattered*, where I unpack this image of the "house of religion" more fully.

9. On these different types of love, see C. S. Lewis's *The Four Loves*.

at paradigmatic lovers in the world it is also possible to catch a glimpse of God by looking *with* such agape lovers, to look where they are looking.

An example of this would be looking at the life of someone like Mother Teresa. One cannot do this for very long without just looking *at* her but looking *with* her, which leads us to try to figure out the motivation for such radical, servant love. Where were her eyes fixed? To try to see with Mother Teresa's eyes is to try to look at the God that she is beholding, the God that generates such agape love within her. This is why the saints are somehow depicted as transparent to God. Looking at them, one can catch glimpses of God.[10]

The "everyday" saints of our own local communities are, however, sometimes even more accessible to our imaginations, and can be even more vivid examples of embodied love. The postal worker who takes time to serve as a "big brother," the busy lawyer who will make time to cook for a church funeral, the teacher who paints houses of poor people for free— all of these people are "laying down their lives" as the 1 John passage calls us to do. Some lives are laid down all at once; others are laid down on a daily basis over eighty-five years. One thing is clear, though—when we look *at* such lives for any time at all, we end up looking *with* them for the source of their inspiration and power.

If preachers can get their hearers to look *through* their examples so as to target the One who makes such lives possible, they will have done their job.

Counseling and Pastoral Care that Shapes the Heart

On Wesley's view of heart religion, pastoral care can be seen as inviting the counselee to target—or re-target—his/her heart on God and the things of God, and to make clear the kind of behaviors that our re-targeted hearts then dispose us to engage in. This obviously entails understanding what objects currently define the heart and mind of the Christian seeking guidance. Wesley's classical question, "how is it with your soul?" can be the

---

10. As mentioned above, Wesley published many biographies of role model Methodists in the early *Arminian Magazine* of the Methodist movement, so we should not fall into the mistake of thinking that considering the lives of saints is only a "Roman Catholic" thing to do.

deceptively simple, yet powerful, way into the subtle art of defining, or redefining, these objects.

Pastors today can perhaps update Wesley's question, with its increasingly anachronistic reference to "soul," by asking questions such as:

- Is your heart marked by *love*? If so, is it the agape love of 1 Corinthians 13 or 1 John 3:16? Or is it a self-seeking, pleasure orientation? When you target your neighbor for love, is it the behaviors of 1 Corinthians 13 (patience, kindness, etc.) that are elicited? Do you target only those who love you, or is it just as often the stranger, the poor, the widow and the orphan?

- What about *joy*? Do you find deep joy only when the sport's team you root for wins? Or do you think you will achieve joy only when you get the next promotion? Or when your stock portfolio hits the magic number? Or do you take joy where Christ said it can truly be found, in humble service?

- Is your *peace* a simple absence of conflict where you float in a void of disconnection, or is it the peace of *shalom*, a positive presence that comes from being in right relationship with God and neighbor?

John Wesley often summarized holiness by referring to the famous "fruit of the spirit" passage in Gal 5:22–24 where this fruit is described as "love, joy, peace, patience, kindness, generosity, faithfulness, gentleness and self control. There is no law against such things" (NRSV). The questions we just asked about love, joy and peace can be asked about all of these "fruit of the spirit." When one is turning one's eyes from the things of the world (which lead to the "works of the flesh," to use Paul's language in Galatians) to the things of God, then these emotions will take their right objects and grow as they should.

Here is where our histories come into play, for our histories tell the story of how the dispositions of our hearts have come to be formed in us. Because of the unique history of each individual person, each will follow a different path to achieving this vision of holiness. Some will start their quest with their hearts defined by a dream of a big payoff from the Lotto. Some will begin their journey with hopes of worldly prestige, or unlimited sexual fulfillment. These starting places must be frankly acknowledged before the transformation can begin, so that these empty, worldly, yearnings can be left on the porch of repentance before we go through the door of faith and into the house of holiness.

The person who is trained to think of him- or herself as superior to all others, for example, will have a different pattern of formation—and, accordingly, a different pattern of *trans*formation that must be undertaken—from the person who was raised to think that he or she has no worth at all. The end point, the *telos*—i.e., the sanctified life of the fruit of the Holy Spirit leading to life eternal—will be the same for both, but the paths from their existing predispositions to that end point will be quite different, with different emphases on different aspects of the Good News.

The egotist needs to be less self-absorbed and more focused on God and the needs of the world, while the person with no self-esteem may be so oriented to self-denial that she has completely lost sight of her self and has forgotten (if she ever knew) that she is a precious child of God, someone for whom Christ died. While the former person needs to stop the idolatry of self, the latter needs to see that one can only give oneself away if one *has* a self, and that selfless service must be consciously and joyously undertaken, and not just guiltily or drearily assumed, if it is truly to honor God and express the Christian heart. If we offer them Christ as the true object of their hearts, both people can reinterpret their individual histories in light of the Good news. Their courses of development will differ, but by God's grace they will meet at the same end point of humble holiness. If we keep our eyes on the God who is revealed through Christ, the God revealed in the Christian Scriptures, if we let the story of salvation become our story by using the means of grace and living the works of piety, then our hearts become changed.

This means that a particular pattern of confession and repentance must be lived out for each individual. For Wesley, it was in the small group— the small groups that were the "classes" or "bands" of his day—where this *particular and personal* confession and repentance can be made to stick, through the loving accountability of our fellow Christians.[11] Regardless of their different starting places, though, all will need a glimpse of the Kingdom of God, a vision of the Risen One who conquered death, so

---

11. See the work of David Lowes Watson in *Early Methodist Class Meetings* and *Accountable Discipleship* for how this process worked in Wesley's time and how it can work today.

that they can "set their hearts on things above and not on things below." Sometimes this kind of pastoral care "re-targeting" and re-interpreting is accomplished by the Holy Spirit without human intervention, but sometimes the Spirit will use a willing human to help in the process. In either case, naming the habitual objects of our hearts—and our habitual dispositions that flow from them—and then re-orienting those hearts to God and the things of God is the essence of the task.

An Example: Targeting our Hearts After a Tragedy

When I was serving as a chaplain on the scene of a plane crash, I saw many concrete instances of how our individual histories need to be first acknowledged, and then interpreted through the filter of the good news.[12] For instance, when dealing with those who had lost love ones, or who had experienced great pain or suffering themselves as a result of this plane crash, it was important to get them to acknowledge the open-ended and open-textured nature of life, both as we experience it, and as the Bible paints it.

When I refer to the "open-ended and open-textured nature of life" I am pointing out that the Bible does not consistently assert that life is going to be fair and neat and without tragedy. The Bible instead presents life as filled with mysteries, blind alleys and brokenness, and yet we also see God working in the midst of that mystery and tragedy to bring about healing and God's purposes.

Take, for instance, the Garden of Eden. It is nowhere explained in the Bible why there is a snake that can bring about temptation in the Garden. The Bible does not try to explain why the snake is there, it just seemingly asserts: "this is the way life is—there are abundant temptations to sin." Similarly, in the book of Job we see the tragedies of life painted in exquisite detail, and yet never explained. Jumping ahead to the New Testament, we see the real persecution of Jesus and his followers and his horrible suffering death on a cross. Instead of explaining this away, scripture calls its readers to take up their crosses and follow him. These heart-breaking realities are not downplayed or soft-pedaled in Scripture. Neither are they given full, metaphysical explanations. When Jesus's disciples asked him if

12. See my theological reflections on tragedy that grew out of this experience in *When the World Breaks Your Heart*.

the people who had a tower fall on them were any worse than anybody else, Jesus simply says "No." There was no philosophizing or trying to explain these things in simple moralistic terms (Luke 13:4).

Inviting the broken-hearted to ponder such passages from the scriptures can take the people who are suffering tragedy and install them into the Biblical world. There, they can see that they are not alone, that they are part of a long and deep tradition of understanding the world that does not mock the broken-hearted or think that because they suffer that they must be harboring some "secret sin." The believers are instead part of a tradition where God's servants "weep with those who weep"[13] and try to bind up the wounds of the hurting.

It is also important to remind the sufferers that it is only for the *believer* that tragedy truly makes sense *as tragedy*. If all of reality were just random atoms with no necessary pattern of meaning, then why should not hearts be broken? If there is no God, then there is no reason for righteous anger—that "accusation of wrongdoing" (see chapter 2). No, it is the Christian who is called to a life of agape love who does not abandon the broken-hearted, but sits beside them and says "I see the same crushing reality that you do, and your anger, despair and sense of outrage are how our hearts *should* interpret this tragedy." It is those who look for a pattern of meaning who find themselves broken—and heart-broken— when they encounter tragedy in their own lives. The open-textured and broken-hearted visions of the world that scripture gives us can be mapped onto the individual person's own experience of the world in settings of pastoral care—or believer-to-believer caring—and the suffering person's participation in God's grand story can be made clear by inviting them to attend to—to set their hearts on—that story.

God's bringing about God's purposes in spite of the evil in the world is paradigmatically seen in the resurrection of Christ. Offering the broken-hearted this vision of the crucified and risen Son of God can help such people both own their own experiences and see them in a Christian way. Knowing that our vision of reality—which paints a picture of a sinful, broken, hate-filled world—is also the vision of reality that the Bible paints, can be a life-giving first step toward healing and a life of grateful discipleship. For it is only if we do not deny the broken and sinful reality

13. Rom 12:15.

that people experience in the everyday life of their hearts that people will be open to hearing the Good News about God's grace and love. It is only after we own our sins, and confess them, and own our wounds, and ask to be made whole, that the wounded healer can bring our redemption and healing.

Wesleyan Evangelism and its Contemporary Rivals

Wesley's comprehensive view of the evangelistic task was well-summarized by Albert Outler in his *Evangelism in the Wesleyan Spirit* where he describes Wesley's conviction that

> Conversion is never more than the bare threshold of authentic and comprehensive evangelism . . . 'never encourage the devil by snatching souls from him that you cannot nurture' . . . Thus, sanctification became the goal and end of all valid evangelistic endeavor (and this implies a lifelong process).[14]

This means that evangelism is really a lifelong process of being continually conformed to the image of God, a lifelong project of renewing the heart, or "spiritual formation."

"Spiritual formation" is a term of long standing in the Roman Catholic tradition, and has become increasing used in Protestant circles in the last thirty years. The idea of an ongoing, life-long process of shaping and "forming" human souls into a predetermined image is certainly consistent with Roman Catholic understanding of grace completing nature—as it is consistent with a Wesleyan vision. I think it is a manifestation of the Wesleyan theological tradition that the Academies for Spiritual Formation as a formal model of deepening our discipleship developed within the United Methodist Church.[15]

Unfortunately, though, there are some contemporary understandings of "spiritual formation" that work against such a clear sense of shaping, patterning, molding, and forming along Christian lines. One of these we might term the "turn within."

14. Outler, *Evangelism in the Wesleyan Spirit*, 23.

15. For more information, see the Upper Room Website (http://www.upperroom.org) and go to the "Academy for Spiritual Formation."

This "turn within" is sometimes joined with Jungian archetypal language, but sometimes it does not have such deep theoretical roots. In any case, this "New Agey" approach to spirituality is to "go within," to "discover the God within," and to realize our potential, by unpacking and unfolding "the gift that we are." It is this kind of spirituality which can obviously turn into an unhelpful emphasis on "feelings" (instead of the underlying emotions), and this can turn narcissistic at the drop of a hat.

It should be equally obvious that this kind of spirituality can lead to a life lived quite readily without ever encountering the Good News. The fact that we are created in the image of God, yet are sinful; that we are someone for whom Christ died; that we are someone whose sins are forgiven; that we are called into a particular and contingent pattern of life marked by the fruit of the Spirit—all of this will never necessarily be encountered by a "turning within," unless the Good News has been placed "in there" already through some process of formation.

While it is important to understand the person that we have become—to understand the nature of our pattern of loyalties, affections, loves and hates, by taking stock of oneself with an "internal" inventory—without an encounter with the gospel that comes from "without" as good news, the seeker will have no way of labeling and understanding one's own heart and history, much less will the seeker have the ability to appropriate God's forgiveness and to grow in the fruit of the spirit.

Aside from this misleading portrayal of Christian spiritual formation—a portrayal that can lead *away from* evangelism and the process of conversion and simply affirm whatever is "within"—there is another particularly troubling feature of our current intellectual culture that can inhibit the process of disciple-making in the Wesleyan tradition. That is the prevailing popular attitude of relativism. I mean the word "popular" in two different ways. First of all, "popular" implies "wide spread," and that is certainly true when it comes to relativism (as is apparent to any one who teaches freshman in college in America today!).

But I also mean "popular" in the sense of "non-professional," since only lay people who have not given it much careful thought can truly embrace such a view. Philosophers, who of necessity must give serious thought to such things, have decisively examined relativism and found it to be intellectually bankrupt. I think it is important to understand some of these reasons for the bankruptcy of relativism if the Wesleyan

Christian call to conversion and intentional formation is to take hold in our churches.

As made clear in philosophical essays such as "Who's to Judge?" by Louis Pojman,[16] the popular idea that "values are determined by the group"—in other words, that right and wrong are defined sociologically—has several specific problems. First of all, when trying to determine what is right and wrong on this model, we find ourselves in an insuperable dilemma because no one belongs to one group only. Which group am I to look to: my family, my country, my fraternity, my church? Within each group, how do I determine truth—call for a vote and let the majority opinion be called "truth?" This would imply that right or wrong is determined by 50 percent plus one.

While this might seem to be just the sort of quandary that relativists would be happy to leave us with, few relativists are in the end happy to settle for the absolute nihilism and anarchy that such a view yields. This is so because if ethical relativism were true, ethical error by a majority would be impossible: by definition, the majority of the group cannot be wrong. One of the implications of this is that reformers are by definition always wrong, since reformers typically start off as a minority in the group. If relativism were right, reformers, and anyone who held a minority view, would be by necessity ruled out of any question of moral deliberation. Even those who embrace an easy relativistic stance are not comfortable with this implication of their view—once it is pointed out to them.

Often, appeals to relativism are made with an equally strong appeal to "tolerance." The problem with this, however, is that tolerance is not a virtue in all groups, societies or cultures. To assume that tolerance is a culturally-neutral, universally accepted value is simply wrong, as anyone trying to evangelize in a predominantly Muslim country is quick to find out—for such activity can lead to a death sentence. Tolerance is embraced by the relativist as something that should have self-evidential power for all people, but tolerance turns out to be a virtue of only certain groups in certain societies.

This does not mean we should promote intolerance, but it simply makes the point that if all affections and values are tied to certain stories, contexts and cultures, then we must not go the route of relativists and say

---

16. See Pojman, "Who's to Judge?"

that any group is as good as any other when it comes to determining what is right of wrong. Instead, we must take the hard task of examining the particular and contingent claims to truth, the particular and contingent ways of life generated by different understandings of reality, and arrive at our own humble—but none the less decisive—conclusions.

We must not so privilege "tolerance" that we hide behind that shibboleth as a way of avoiding the hard and humbling task of discernment. We can never be so paralyzed by a fear of intolerance that we lose our fear of living in error. If we were to follow the road of the relativists, we would have to accede to the proposition that, for instance, the Utku people (discussed in chapter 2) with their lack of anger and their sense of fatalism, are living a life spiritually equivalent to one that allowed for transformative action motivated by a sense of wrongdoing and injustice.

This is not to say that we should close ourselves off from receiving further information or jettison any possibility of changing our minds once we are committed to our vision of truth. One of the features of the Christian way of life, after all, is humility, and this implies empathetic openness to the views of others. But understanding that relativism offers no easy escape from the need for embracing *some* model for human change *does* mean that confident commitment to fostering change according to a particular model—Christian conversion and spiritual formation—must be a non-negotiable feature of the life of our churches.[17]

Emphasizing a lifetime of sanctification, the Wesleyan tradition places the drama of human change on center stage every day of life, not only at a one-time event. In this context, then, we can come to understand, and appreciate the role of, "spiritual formation" in the life-long task of being "renewed in the image of God."

---

17. The easy, popular acceptance of relativism does show some signs of cracking. Regarding certain issues that some constituencies regard as non-negotiable, the problems with relativism have come to the surface. See the recent discussion about female circumcision in Africa and whether or not speaking out against such practices is "culturally imperialistic" and "paternalistic" or whether such interventions on behalf of women are morally justified. For example, Perlez, "Uganda's Women."

Evangelism and The Competing Ways of Life of Galatians 5

For Wesley, as for all biblically-based theologians, the stark contrast between the "fruit of the Spirit" and the "works of the flesh" illustrates decisively both the need for conversion and the need for an intentional pattern of post-conversion growth. To say "yes" to one particular pattern of formation is to say "no" to all competing ways of life and that is the undeniable element of conversion in the Christian life. As Paul makes clear, there is no middle ground between the "works of the flesh" (such as impurity, licentiousness, idolatry, enmities, strife, jealousy, anger and envy) and the "fruit of the Spirit" (which include love, joy, peace, patience, kindness, generosity, faithfulness, gentleness, and self-control).

When witnessing to the unconverted, it is especially important to understand that *both* what Christianity *affirms* as a flourishing way of life (the fruit of the Spirit) and what it *works against* (sinfulness or the works of the flesh) are defined *within* the Christian story. Christians need not assume that what they call "sin" is seen as such by the rest of the world. In that sense, the pattern for the Christian way of life, defined by orthodoxy, orthopraxis and orthokardia, is not some sort of universally achievable insight that can be gotten by merely introspecting. Christianity is a contingent way of life, formed by taking very particular narratives as the object of one's consciousness, and being formed according to those narratives. Conversion, thus entails not only a positive vision of the image into which we are to grow, but also a re-configuring of what we need to grow away *from*. We do not know what sin is, in short, until we know what grace and salvation are. As Karl Barth reputedly once said, "We don't even know what questions to ask until we hear the answers."

Taking this view of things does two important things. It shows the limits of "natural theology," especially those forms of introspecting on the supposedly "given" human experience that mark the methods of "new age" seekers, and it allows for a quality of Christian proclamation which is all-too-often sadly missing today—a humble confidence.

One of the benefits of Wesley's construal of the evangel as necessarily leading to a sanctified life is that *a way of life* can be proclaimed—and embodied—with confidence in the contemporary world. Leander Keck in the *Church Confident* has struck on one of the key problems in the life of the church of our day when he says that all too often our church's confused self-understanding and murky theology have prevented us from speaking the Good News with *confidence*. A way of life is something that can be directly observed and is directly accessible to the world and, therefore, constitutes a peculiarly confident witness.

When the Christian way of life, (described by all three of the "orthos") is embodied in real life believers, there is in fact no more confident proclamation possible. If our clearest message is a debatable metaphysic, a plea for a certain view about the Bible, a set of political positions, or a narrow moralism, then our confidence will always lie in something other than the incarnated redeeming power of the Holy Spirit. If we live out of a renewed heart that comes from targeting God, others, when they see our lives, will have a concrete, formidable and imitable example for their own call to love God.

Calling for conversion—calling for a new way of life—goes against the current trends of privileging unity and commonality. Talk of "conversion" seems to some necessarily to smack of divisiveness and even judgmentalism. But as Christians we also need to remember that there is no neutral commonality between the fruit of the spirit and the works of the flesh. To try to split the difference between these two life options is not high-minded compromise, but the folly proscribed by Scripture when it describes those who are neither hot nor cold—which leads to being spit out of the mouth (Rev 3:15–16). Christians must always claim that our unity lies in Christ, not in the timid fear of offending someone's prejudices. Our unity lies in the truth of the gospel made real in a renewed heart, a gospel humbly and lovingly proclaimed and lived out in the midst of the sinful and broken world.

A Final Word: The Fundamental Challenge to a Ministry of Shaping Hearts

Perhaps the most challenging feature of this vision of the Christian life that Wesley offers us—this vision of the renewed heart as the goal of sanctification—is the need for those calling for this change *to be changed themselves.* The people who are leading the call for renewal, whether it be an ordained leader in the congregation or a layperson who is trying to witness at work, will become the most obvious targets for the attention of the lay people. Those most prominent will often be the objects on which people will fix their attention. People will, for example, look to see where the minister's eyes are fixed, to see what behaviors he or she is disposed towards, in order to try to catch a glimpse of Christ. Religious language is a difficult idiom because it demands so much from the speaker.

While serving as a model in this way can be so daunting as to seem an impossible role for anyone to fill, one must remember that Christ invites us to enter into the kingdom with the humility of children.[18] Humility means knowing that we are not God, and that we merely are trying to use the freedom God has given us to cooperate with the Holy Spirit. Only when we have a vivid awareness of this humility that comes from daily crossing the "porch of repentance" can God can use us as "spiritual directors"—which on Wesley's terms, all Christians should be—directing the "spiritual senses" of the heart to the ultimate heart shaping narrative, the good news.

This humility must be seen as qualifying *all* of the affections of our own heart, and not just be a passing episode or feeling that we experience every once in a while. One of Wesley's favorite summaries of the whole life of holiness was "humble love." If we think that we have God fully captured in the box of our theological formulations, or think we have written some text that provides an irrefutable argument for the truth of Christianity, or even if we think that God is fully revealed in our own lives, we are doing both our fellow Christians and ourselves a disservice. It is only when we serve with humility that we can serve as pointers to the Holy One who was born in a barn and washed the feet of others.

"Offer them Christ," then, is not just a slogan to authorize preaching or evangelism, but it is the basic charge of all Christian ministries. When we offer them Christ, and cooperate with God in the process of incarnating God's Holy Spirit in our own lives, we invite the people to target their hearts on God and the things of God. When people thus focus their attention on their one, true heart's desire, they can discern the joyful work of obedience to which their renewed hearts dispose them.

Finally, then, the most persuasive evangelistic appeal to the world is found in the quality of our lives. If we are truly happy in the deep philosophical (and Wesleyan) sense of *eudaemonism*, and that happiness is visible in our lives through humble love of God and neighbor, then others

18. Matt 18:3–4.

will see it in our lives and will want it for themselves. Living enfleshed happiness, seen in the life of the renewed heart, can lead others to claim holiness as their *telos* as well. When we live that vision in the midst of our broken and sinful world, conversion and the renewal of hearts in the image of God will occur.

Wesley thought that the most persuasive evidence for the power of the gospel to change hearts is the existence of such gospel-renewed hearts and lives. Against this witness, there can be no refutation. In fact, the most appropriate response to such a witness is not any form of argument—it is imitation.

Bibliography

Primary Sources

The Works of John Wesley. Began as "The Oxford Edition of the Works of John Wesley." Oxford: Clarendon, 1975–1983; continued as "The Bicentennial Edition of the Works of John Wesley." Nashville: Abingdon, 1984–.

The Works of The Rev. John Wesley. 3rd ed. Edited by Thomas Jackson. 14 vols. London: Wesleyan-Methodist Book Room, 1829–1831. Reprinted, Grand Rapids: Zondervan, 1958; Grand Rapids: Baker, 1979. Abbreviated as Jackson Works.

The Letters of John Wesley. Edited by John Telford. 8 vols. London: Epworth, 1931.

Explanatory Notes Upon the New Testament. London: William Bowyer, 1755. Reprinted, London: Epworth, 1976. Abbreviated as *N.T. Notes.*

Explanatory Notes Upon the Old Testament. Bristol: William Pine, 1765. Reprinted, Salem, OH: Schmul, 1975. Abbreviated as *O.T. Notes.*

"Thoughts on the Sin of Onan." London: 1767.

Secondary Sources

Abraham, William J. *Canon and Criterion in Christian Theology: From the Fathers to Feminism.* New York: Oxford University Press, 1998.

———. "The Concept of Inspiration in the Classical Wesleyan Tradition." In *A Celebration of Ministry,* edited by Kenneth C. Kinghorn, 33–47. Wilmore, KY: Asbury Seminary Press, 1982.

———. "The End of Wesleyan Theology." *Wesleyan Theological Journal* 40 (2005) 7–25.

———. *The Logic of Evangelism.* Grand Rapids: Eerdmans, 1989.

———. *Waking from Doctrinal Amnesia: The Healing of Doctrine in the United Methodist Church.* Nashville: Abingdon, 1995.

Arnott, Felix R. "Anglicanism in the Seventeenth Century." In *Anglicanism: The Thought and Practice of the Church of England,* edited by Paul Elmer More and Frank Leslie Cross, lvii. New York: Macmillan, 1935.

Augustine. *On Christian Doctrine.* Translated by D. W. Robertson. New York: Bobbs-Merrill, 1958.

Ayling, Stanley. *John Wesley.* Nashville: Abingdon, 1979.

Baker, Frank. "The Beginnings of American Methodism." *Methodist History* 2 (1963) 1–15.

———. *John Wesley and the Church of England.* Nashville: Abingdon, 1970.

———. "A Study of John Wesley's Readings." *London Quarterly and Holborn Review* 168 (1943) 140–45 and 234–42.

Baker, Frank, editor. *A Union Catalogue of the Publications of John and Charles Wesley.* Durham, NC: Divinity School, Duke University, 1966.

Bass, Dorothy C., editor. *Practicing Our Faith: A Way of Life for a Searching People.* San Francisco: Jossey-Bass, 1997.

Blankenship, Paul F. "The Significance of John Wesley's Abridgement of the Thirty-Nine Articles as Seen from his Deletions." *Methodist History* 2:3 (1964) 35–47.

Bonhoeffer, Dietrich. *Letters and Papers from Prison.* Edited by Eberhard Bethge. Translated by Reginald H. Fuller. New York: Macmillan, 1972.

Booth, Wayne C. *The Dogma of Modern Assent.* Chicago: University of Chicago Press, 1974.

Boshears, Onva K. "John Wesley, the Bookman: A Study of His Reading Interests in the Eighteenth Century." PhD diss., University of Michigan, 1972.

Brantley, Richard E. *Locke, Wesley, and the Method of English Romanticism.* Gainesville: University of Florida Press, 1984.

Brown, Dale. *Understanding Pietism.* Grand Rapids: Eerdmans, 1978.

Burtner, R. W., and R. E. Chiles, editors. *A Compend of Wesley's Theology.* New York: Abingdon, 1954.

Campbell, Ted. "John Wesley's Conceptions and Uses of Christian Antiquity." PhD diss., Southern Methodist University, 1984.

———. *Methodist Doctrine: The Essentials.* Nashville: Abingdon, 1999.

———. Unpublished papers delivered at the Manchester Wesley Tercentenary Conference, June 18, 2003, and at "The Legacy of John Wesley for the Twenty-First Century" Conference, held at Asbury Theological Seminary October, 1–3, 2003.

Cannon, William R. "John Wesley's Doctrine of Sanctification and Perfection." *Mennonite Quarterly Review* 35 (1961) 91–95.

———. "Salvation in the Theology of John Wesley." *Methodist History* 9 (1970) 3–12.

Cannon, William R. *The Theology of John Wesley.* New York: Abingdon, 1946.

Casto, Robert Michael. "Exegetical Method in John Wesley's *Explanatory Notes Upon the Old Testament:* A Description of his Approach, Use of Sources, and Practice." PhD diss., Duke University, 1977.

Cell, George C. *The Rediscovery of John Wesley.* New York: Holt, 1935.

Charry, Ellen. *By The Renewing of Our Minds: The Pastoral Function of Christian Doctrine.* New York: Oxford University Press, 1997.

Cherry, Charles Conrad. *The Theology of Jonathan Edwards: A Reappraisal.* Garden City, NY: Anchor, 1966.

Chilcote, Paul Wesley, editor. *The Wesleyan Tradition: A Paradigm for Renewal.* Nashville: Abingdon, 2002.

———. *Recapturing the Wesleys Vision: An Introduction to the Faith of John and Charles Wesley.* Downers Grove: InterVarsity, 2004.

———. "The Women Pioneers of Early Methodism." In *Wesleyan Theology Today: A Bicentennial Theological Consultation,* edited by Theodore Runyon, 180–84. Nashville: Kingswood, 1985.

Clapper, Gregory S. *As if the Heart Mattered: A Wesleyan Spirituality*. Nashville: Upper Room, 1997.

——. "Finding a Place for Emotions in Christian Theology." *Christian Century*, April 29, 1987.

——. "From the 'Works of the Flesh' to the 'Fruit of the Spirit:' Conversion and Spiritual Formation in the Wesleyan Tradition." In *Conversion in the Wesleyan Tradition*, edited by Kenneth J. Collins and John H. Tyson, 211–22. Nashville: Abingdon, 2001.

——. "Is Love an Affection or an Emotion? Looking at Wesley's Heart Language in a New Light." In *The Many Facets of Love: Philosophical Explorations*, edited by Thomas Jay Oord, 75–84. Newcastle: Cambridge Scholars Publishing, 2007.

——. *John Wesley on Religious Affections: His Views on Experience and Emotion and their Role in the Christian Life and Theology*. Metuchen, NJ: Scarecrow, 1989.

——. *Living Your Heart's Desire: God's Call and Your Vocation*. Nashville: Upper Room, 2005.

——. "Making Disciples in Community: Guidance and Transformation in the Living Body of Believers." In *The Wesleyan Tradition: A Paradigm for Renewal*, edited by Paul Chilcote, 118–22. Nashville: Abingdon, 2002.

——. "*Orthokardia*: The Practical Theology of John Wesley's Heart Religion." *Quarterly Review* 10 (1990) 49–66.

——. "Relations Between Theology and Spirituality: Kierkegaard's Model." *Studies in Formative Spirituality* 9 (1988) 161–67.

——. "Shaping Heart Religion through Preaching and Pastoral Care." In *"Heart Religion" in the Methodist Tradition and Related Movements*, 209–24. Lanham, MD: Scarecrow, 2001.

——. "'True Religion' and the Affections: A Study of John Wesley's Abridgement of Jonathan Edwards' *Treatise on Religious Affections*." In *Wesleyan Theology Today: A Bicentennial Theological Consultation*, edited by Theodore Runyon, 416–23. Nashville: Kingswood, 1985.

——. "Wesley's Language of the Heart." *Wesleyan Theological Journal* 44:2 (2009) forthcoming.

——. "Wesley's 'Main Doctrines:' Spiritual Formation and Teaching in the Wesleyan tradition." *Wesleyan Theological Journal* 39:2 (2004) 97–121.

——. *When the World Breaks Your Heart: Spiritual Ways of Living with Tragedy*. Nashville: Upper Room, 1999.

Clebsch, William A. "The Sensible Spirituality of Jonathan Edwards." In *American Religious Thought: A History*, 11–56. Chicago: University of Chicago Press, 1973.

Collins, Kenneth J. "John Wesley's Topography of the Heart: Dispositions, Tempers and Affections." *Methodist History* 36:3 (1998) 162–75.

——. *The Theology of John Wesley: Holy Love and the Shape of Grace*. Nashville: Abingdon, 2007.

Collins, Kenneth J., and J. H. Tyson, editors. *Conversion in the Wesleyan Tradition*. Nashville: Abingdon, 2001.

Cottingham, John. *The Spiritual Dimension: Religion, Philosophy and Human Value*. Cambridge: Cambridge University Press, 2005

——. *The Church and the Age of Reason, 1648–1789*. Harmondsworth: Penguin, 1960.

Cragg, Gerald R. *Reason and Authority in the Eighteenth Century*. Cambridge: Cambridge University Press, 1964.

Davies, Rupert, and Gordon Rupp, editors. *A History of the Methodist Church in Great Britain.* 2 vols. London: Epworth, 1965.

Delattre, Roland A. *Beauty and Sensibility in the Thought of Jonathan Edwards: An Essay in Aesthetics and Theological Ethics.* New Haven: Yale University Press, 1968.

Deschner, John. *Wesley's Christology: An Interpretation.* Dallas: Southern Methodist University Press, 1985.

Dixon, Thomas. *From Passions to Emotions: The Creation of a Secular Psychological Category.* Cambridge: Cambridge University Press, 2003.

Dreyer, Frederick. "Faith and Experience in the Thought of John Wesley." *The American Historical Review* 88 (1982) 12–30.

Dryer, Elizabeth. *Passionate Spirituality: Hildegard of Bingen and Hadewijch of Brabant.* New York: Paulist, 2005

Dykstra, Craig. *Growing in the Life of Faith: Education and Christian Practices.* Louisville: Geneva, 1999.

Edwards, Jonathan. *The Works of Jonathan Edwards.* 25 vols. Edited by Perry Miller. New Haven: Yale University Press, 1957–2006.

———. Vol. 1, *Freedom of the Will.* Edited by Paul Ramsey, 1957.

———. Vol. 2, *Religious Affections.* Edited by John E. Smith, 1959.

———. Vol. 3, *Original Sin.* Edited by Clyde A. Holbrook, 1970.

———. Vol. 4, *The Great Awakening.* Edited by C. C. Goen, 1972.

———. Vol. 5, *Apocalyptic Writings.* Edited by Stephen J. Stein, 1977.

———. Vol. 6, *Scientific and Philosophic Writings.* Edited by Wallace E. Anderson, 1980.

Erdt, Terence. "The Calvinist Psychology of the Heart and the 'Sense' of Jonathan Edwards." *Early American Literature* 13 (1978) 165–80.

———. *Jonathan Edwards: Art and the Sense of the Heart.* Amherst: University of Massachusetts Press, 1980.

Feuerbach, Ludwig. *The Essence of Christianity.* Foreword by H. Richard Niebuhr. Introduction by Karl Barth. New York: Harper Torchbook, 1957.

Fiering, Norman. *Jonathan Edwards' Moral Thought and Its British Context.* Chapel Hill: University of North Carolina Press, 1981.

Flaubert, Gustave. *Madame Bovary.* Norwalk, CT: Easton, 1978.

Gadamer, Hans-Georg. *Truth and Method.* Translation edited by Garrett Barden and John Cumming. New York: Continuum, 1975.

Glasson, Francis. "Wesley's New Testament Reconsidered." *Epworth Review* (1983) 28–34.

Graver, Margaret R. *Stoicism and Emotion.* Chicago: University of Chicago Press, 2007.

Green, Joel. "Contribute or Capitulate? Wesleyans, Pentecostals, and Reading the Bible in a Post-colonial Mode." *Wesleyan Theological Journal* 39 (2004) 74–90.

Grenz, Stanley. *Revisioning Evangelical Theology: A Fresh Agenda for the 21st Century.* Downers Grove: InterVarsity, 1993.

Griffiths, Paul E. *What Emotions Really Are: The Problem of Psychological Categories.* Chicago: University of Chicago Press, 1997.

Haartman, Keith. *Watching and Praying: Personality Transformation in Eighteenth Century British Methodism.* New York: Rodopi, 2004.

Hall, Thor. "The Christian's Life: Wesley's Alternative to Luther and Calvin" in *Duke Divinity School Bulletin* 28 (1963) 111–26.

Hauerwas, Stanley, Nancey C. Murphy, and Mark Nation, editors. *Theology Without Foundations: Religious Practice and the Future of Theological Truth*. Nashville: Abingdon, 1994.

Hays, Richard B. *Echoes of Scripture in the Letters of Paul*. New Haven: Yale University Pres, 1989.

Heitzenrater, Richard. *The Elusive Mr. Wesley*. 2 vols. Nashville: Abingdon, 1984.

———. *Wesley and the People Called Methodists*. Nashville: Abingdon, 1995.

Herbert, T. W. *John Wesley as Editor and Author*. Princeton: Princeton University Press, 1940.

Hildebrandt, Franz. *From Luther to Wesley*. London: Lutterworth, 1951.

Holifield, Brooks. *The History of Pastoral Care in America*. Nashville, Abingdon, 1983.

Holmer, Paul L. *The Grammar of Faith*. San Francisco: Harper & Row, 1978.

Horst, Mark. "Christian Understanding and the Life of Faith in John Wesley's Thought." PhD diss., Yale University, 1985.

———. "Engendering the Community of Faith in an Age of Individualism: A Review of George Lindbeck's *The Nature of Doctrine: Religion and Theology in a Postliberal Age*." *Quarterly Review* 8 (1988) 89–97.

Horst, Mark. "Wholeness and Method in Wesley's Theology." *Quarterly Review* 7:2 (1987) 11–23.

Hynson, Leon O. *To Reform the Nation: Theological Foundations of Wesley's Ethics*. Grand Rapids: Asbury, 1984.

Jakes, T. D. "The Secret Place." A CD series published by T. D. Jakes Ministry, Dallas, Texas.

Jennings, Theodore W. "John Wesley *Against* Aldersgate." *Quarterly Review* 8:3 (1988) 3–22.

Johnson, Samuel. *A Dictionary of the English Language on CD-ROM*. Edited by Anne McDermott Cambridge: Cambridge University Press, 1996.

Jones, Scott. *United Methodist Doctrine: The Extreme Center*. Nashville: Abingdon, 2002.

Kallstad, Thorvald. *John Wesley and the Bible: A Psychological Perspective*. Stockholm: NY A BokfOrlags Aktiebolaget, 1974.

Keck, Leander. *The Church Confident*. Nashville: Abingdon, 1993.

———. *Paul and His Letters*. Philadelphia: Fortress, 1979.

Kellet, Norman L. "John Wesley and the Restoration of the Doctrine of the Holy Spirit to the Church of England in the Eighteenth Century." PhD diss., Brandeis University, 1975.

Kierkegaard, Søren. *Concluding Unscientific Postscript*. Translated by David F. Swenson; completed after his death and provided with introduction and notes by Walter Lowrie. Princeton: Princeton University Press, 1941.

Klaiber, Walter, and Manfred Marquardt. *Living Grace: An Outline of United Methodist Theology*. Nashville: Abingdon, 2001.

Knight, Henry H. *The Presence of God in the Christian Life*. Metuchen, NJ: Scarecrow, 1992.

Knight, John Allen. "Aspects of Wesley's Theology after 1770." *Methodist History* 6:3 (1968) 33–42.

Knox, R. A. *Enthusiasm: A Chapter in the History of Religion with Special Reference to the 17th and 18th Centuries*. Oxford: Clarendon, 1950.

Langford, Thomas A. *Methodist Theology*. London: Epworth, 1998.

Lauritzen, Paul. *Religious Belief and Emotional Transformation: A Light in the Heart.* Lewisburg: Bucknell University Press, 1992.

Lawson, John. *Notes on Wesley's Forty-Four Sermons.* London: Epworth, 1946.

Lewis, C. S. *The Four Loves.* New York: Harcourt Brace, 1988.

———. *Mere Christianity.* San Francisco: Harper San Francisco, 1952

———. *The Screwtape Letters.* West Chicago: Lord and King, 1976.

Lindbeck, George A. *The Nature of Doctrine: Religion and Theology in a Postliberal Age.* Philadelphia: Westminster, 1984.

Lindstrom, Harald. *Wesley and Sanctification.* London: Epworth, 1950.

Long, D. Stephen. *John Wesley's Moral Theology: The Quest for God and Goodness.* Nashville: Kingswood, 2005.

Lowery, Kevin Twain. *Salvaging Wesley's Agenda: A New Paradigm for Wesleyan Virtue Ethics.* Princeton Theological Monograph Series 86. Eugene, OR: Pickwick, 2008.

Lowrie, Walter. *Kierkegaard.* Gloucester: Peter Smith, 1970.

Lyons, William. *Emotion.* Cambridge: Cambridge University Press, 1980.

MacIntyre, Alasdair. *After Virtue: A Study in Moral Theory.* Notre Dame: Notre Dame Press, 1984.

———. *Whose Justice? Which Rationality?* Notre Dame: Notre Dame Press, 1988.

Maddox, Randy L. "'Celebrating the Whole Wesley': A Legacy for Contemporary Wesleyans." *Methodist History* 43:2 (2005) 74–89.

———. "A Change in Affections: The Development, Dynamics, and Detachment of John Wesley's Heart Religion." In *"Heart Religion" in the Methodist Tradition and Related Movements,* edited by Richard Steele, 3–31. Metuchen, NJ: Scarecrow, 2001.

———. "John Wesley—Practical Theologian?" *Wesleyan Theological Journal* 23:1–2 (1988) 122–47.

———. "Practical Theology: A Discipline in Search of a Definition." *Perspectives in Religious Studies* 18 (1991) 159–69.

———. "The Recovery of Theology as a Practical Discipline." *Theological Studies* 51 (1990) 650–72.

———. *Responsible Grace: John Wesley's Practical Theology.* Nashville: Abingdon, 1994.

———. "Shaping the Virtuous Heart: The Abiding Mission of the Wesleys." *Circuit Rider* 29:4 (2005) 27–28.

———. "'Vital Orthodoxy': A Wesleyan Dynamic for 21st-Century Christianity," *Methodist History* 42 (2003) 3–19.

Manspeaker, Nancy. *Jonathan Edwards: Bibliographical Synopses.* Lewiston, NY: Mellen, 1981.

Marcuse, Herbert. *The Aesthetic Dimension.* Boston: Beacon, 1978.

Marshall, G. D. "On Being Affected." *Mind* 77 (1968) 243–59.

Matthews, Rex D. "Reason, Faith, and Experience in the Thought of John Wesley." A paper presented at the Oxford Institute of Methodist Theological Studies, 1982.

———. "'With the Eyes of Faith': Spiritual Experience and the Knowledge of God in the Theology of John Wesley." In *Wesleyan Theology Today,* edited by Theodore Runyon, 406–15. Nashville: Kingswood, 1985.

McCarthy, Daryl. "Early Wesleyan Views of Scripture." *Wesleyan Theological Journal* 16.2 (1981) 95–105.

McGinn, Bernard. "The Language of Inner Experience in Christian Mysticism." *Spiritus* 1 (2001) 156–71.

Meeks, M. Douglas, editor. *The Future of the Methodist Theological Traditions*. Nashville: Abingdon, 1985.

Meredith, Lawrence. "Essential Doctrine in the Theology of John Wesley, With Special Attention to the Methodist Standards of Doctrine." ThD thesis, Harvard University, 1962.

Miguez Bonino, Jose. *Doing Theology in a Revolutionary Situation*. Philadelphia: Fortress, 1975.

Miller, Perry. *Jonathan Edwards*. New York: Sloane, 1949.

Murphy, Nancey. "A Non-reductive Physicalist Account of Religious Experience." In *Whatever Happened to the Soul?*, edited by Warren Brown et al., 143–48. Minneapolis: Fortress, 1998.

Neu, Jerome. *A Tear Is an Intellectual Thing: The Meanings of Emotion*. New York: Oxford University Press, 2000.

Nussbaum, Martha. *Upheavals of Thought: The Intelligence of Emotions*. Cambridge: Cambridge University Press, 2001.

Outler, Albert C. *The Albert Outler Library*. Anderson, IN: Bristol, 1995

———. *Evangelism in the Wesleyan Spirit*. Nashville: Tidings, 1971.

———. "John Wesley as Theologian—Then and Now." *Methodist History* 12:4 (1974) 63–82.

———. "Methodism's Theological Heritage: A Study in Perspective." In *Methodism's Destiny in the Ecumenical Age*, edited by Paul M. Minus, 44–70. New York: Abingdon, 1969.

———. "Towards a Re-appraisal of John Wesley as a Theologian." *Perkins Journal* 14:2 (1961) 5–14.

———. *Theology in the Wesleyan Spirit*. Nashville: Discipleship Resources, 1975.

———, editor. *John Wesley*. New York: Oxford University Press, 1964.

Outler, Albert C., and Richard Heitzenrater, editors. *John Wesley's Sermons: An Anthology*. Nashville: Abingdon, 1991.

Oxford English Dictionary. 2 vols. Oxford: Oxford University Press, 1971.

Perlez, Jane. "Uganda's Women: Children, Drudgery, and Pain." In *Virtue and Vice in Everyday Life*, 4th ed., edited by Christina Hoff Sommers, 226–31. Ft. Worth: Harcourt Brace, 1997.

Pojman, Louis. "Who's to Judge?" In *Vice and Virtue in Everyday Life*, 5th ed., edited by Christina Hoff Sommers, 237–50. New York: Harcourt College, 2001.

———. *Philosophy of Religion: An Anthology*. Belmont: Wadsworth, 2003.

Proudfoot, Wayne. *Religious Experience*. Berkeley: University of California Press, 1985.

Ricoeur, Paul. *The Conflict of Interpretations*. Evanston: Northwestern University Press, 1974.

Roberts, Robert C. *Emotions: An Essay in Aid of Moral Psychology*. Cambridge: Cambridge University Press, 2003.

———. *Spiritual Emotions: A Psychology of Christian Virtues*. Grand Rapids: Eerdmans, 2007.

———. *Spirituality and Human Emotion*. Grand Rapids: Eerdmans, 1982.

———. *The Strengths of a Christian*. Philadelphia: Westminster, 1984.

———. "Will and Power in the Virtues." In *Vice and Virtue in Everyday Life: Readings in Ethics*, edited by Christina Hoff Sommers and Fred Sommers, 266–88. Ft. Worth: Harcourt Brace, 1993.

Roberts, Robert C., and Jay Woods. *Intellectual Virtues: An Essay in Regulative Epistemology.* Oxford: Oxford University Press, 2007.

Rogers, Charles A. "'The Concept of Prevenient Grace in the Theology of John Wesley," PhD diss., Duke University, 1967.

———. "John Wesley and Jonathan Edwards." *Duke Divinity School Review* 31 (1966) 20–38.

Rowe, Kenneth E. editor. *The Place of Wesley in the Christian Tradition.* Metuchen, NJ: Scarecrow, 1976.

Runyon, Theodore. *The New Creation.* Nashville: Abingdon, 1998.

———. "A New Look at 'Experience.'" *Drew Gateway* (1987) 44–55.

———. *Sanctification and Liberation.* Nashville: Abingdon, 1981.

———. "What Is Methodism's Theological Contribution Today?" In *Wesleyan Theology Today,* 7–14. Nashville: Kingswood, 1985.

———, editor. *Hope for The Church: Moltmann in Dialogue with Practical Theology.* Nashville: Abingdon, 1979.

Rutman, Darrett B., editor. *The Great Awakening.* New York: Wiley, 1970.

Ryle, Gilbert. *The Concept of Mind.* New York: Harper & Row, 1949.

———. "Feelings." *Philosophical Quarterly* 1 (1951) 193–205.

Saliers, Don E. *The Soul in Paraphrase: Prayer and the Religious Affections.* New York: Seabury, 1980. Revised edition, Akron, OH: Order of St. Luke, 2002.

———. *Worship and Spirituality.* Philadelphia: Westminster, 1984.

———. *Worship as Theology: Foretaste of Divine Glory.* Nashville: Abingdon, 1994

Sartre, Jean-Paul. *The Emotions: Outline of a Theory.* New York: Philosophical Library, 1948.

Schleiermacher, F. D. E. *The Christian Faith.* Philadelphia: Fortress, 1976

Scroggs, Robin. "John Wesley as Biblical Scholar." *Journal of Bible and Religion* 28 (1969) 415–22.

Solomon, Robert, and Cheshire Calhoun, editors. *What Is an Emotion?* New York: Oxford University Press, 1984.

Steele, Richard. *"Gracious Affections" and "True Virtue" According to Jonathan Edwards and John Wesley.* Metuchen: Scarecrow, 1994.

———. "Narrative Theology and the Religious Affections." In *Theology Without Foundations: Religious Practice and the Future of Theological Truth,* edited by Stanley Hauerwas, Nancey Murphy, and Mark T. Nation, 163–79. Nashville: Abingdon, 1994.

———, editor. *"Heart Religion" in the Methodist Tradition and Related Movements.* Metuchen: Scarecrow, 2001.

Stendahl, Krister. *Paul Among Jews and Gentiles.* Philadelphia: Fortress, 1976.

Stephen, Leslie. *History of English Thought in the Eighteenth Century.* 2 vols. New York: Putnam, 1902.

———, editor. *Dictionary of National Biography.* New York: Macmillan, 1896.

Stoeffler, F. Ernest. "Pietism, the Wesleys, and Methodist Beginnings in America." In *Continental Pietism and Early American Christianity,* 184–221. Grand Rapids: Eerdman's, 1976.

Thomas, Owen C. "Interiority and Christian Spirituality." *The Journal of Religion* 80 (2000) 41–60.

Tyson, John R. "Essential Doctrines and Real Religion: Theological Method in Wesley's Sermons on Several Occasions." *Wesleyan Theological Journal* 23 (1988) 163–79.

Volf, Miroslav, and Dorothy Bass, editors. *Practicing Theology: Beliefs, and Practices in Christian Life*. Grand Rapids: Eerdmans, 2002 .

Wainwright, Geoffrey. Review *Wesley's Christology*, by John Deschner. *Perkins Journal* 39:2 (1986) 55–56.

Wainwright, William J. *Reason and the Heart: A Prolegomenon to a Critique of Passional Reason*. Ithaca: Cornell University Press, 1995.

Watson, David Loews. *Accountable Discipleship*. Nashville: Discipleship Resources, 1986.

———. *The Early Methodist Class Meeting: Its Origins and Significance*. Nashville: Discipleship Resources, 1985.

White, James F. *John Wesley's Sunday Service*. Quarterly Review Reprint Series. 1984.

Williams, Colin W. *John Wesley's Theology Today*. New York: Abingdon, 1960.

Wuthnow, Robert. "Spiritual Practice." *The Christian Century*, September 23–30, 1998, 854–55.

Wynkoop, Mildred Bangs. *A Theology of Love*. Kansas City: Beacon Hill, 1972.

Wynn, Mark R. *Emotional Experience and Religious Understanding: Integrating Perception, Conception and Feeling*. Cambridge: Cambridge University Press, 2005.

Index

Abraham, 21

Abraham, William, 102, 103

accountability, 122

Acts 7:23, 56; 13:22, 21; 15:9, 21; 15:29, 78; 16:7, 56; 17:18, 56; 17:27, 55; 18:5, 56; 17:32, 25; 20:37, 56; 22:3, 22; 23:3, 71; 27:23, 77; 28:6, 25

adjectives and adverbs as showing genuine faith, 96

adultery, 21, 97

affectiones, 34

affection(s), 3, 4, 6, 7, 9, 12, 13, 14, 16, 20, 22, 24, 25, 26, 27, 29, 30, 33, 34, 35, 36, 37, 38, 43, 47, 48, 51, 52, 53, 54, 57, 58, 59, 60, 61, 62, 63, 65, 66, 68, 69, 70, 71, 72, 73, 74, 75, 76, 77, 78, 79, 80, 81, 82, 83, 84, 85, 86, 87, 88, 92, 95, 97, 98, 101, 102, 105, 106, 107, 108, 109, 116, 117, 126, 127, 131

affections and self-deception, 78–80

affections as needing society/community, 76–88

affections as object-related/transitive, 68–76

affections differentiated from emotions, 33–38

affectivity, 20, 36, 39, 44, 47, 51, 52, 58, 65, 71, 75, 83, 84

affectus, 34

agape, 113, 119, 120, 121, 124

Aldersgate, 7, 64

angels, 34, 35, 78

anger, 35, 43, 44, 49, 50, 82, 124, 128, 129

appetite(s), 34, 35, 84

Aquinas, Thomas, 34, 35, 43, 84, 105

Aristotle, 10, 43

Arminian Magazine, 102, 109, 120

assurance, 58–61

Augustine, 34, 35, 78, 105

ayuqnaq (Utku concept of fatalism), 50

Babette's Feast, 110

Bailey, George, 110, 119

bands, 86, 116, 122

Barth, Karl, 28, 75, 87, 129

Bass, Dorothy C., 93, 94, 99

beatitudes, 10, 12

beliefs leading to emotional transformation, 47–51

Bible on the heart and its renewal, 17–30

bios changing to *zoe* as the purpose of Christianity, 27

Bonhoeffer, Dietrich, 87

Booth, Wayne, 86

Brantley, Richard, 69

broken/brokenness, 108, 111, 113, 123, 124, 130, 132

Brown, Thomas, 36, 37

Browne, Peter, 69

Bundy, David, 4

Campbell, Ted, 6, 99

Casto, Robert, 10, 11, 17

Cavenac, Monsieur, 51

Chalmers, Thomas, 36

"Character of a Methodist, The," 83

charity, 34, 81, 110

Charry, Ellen, 26, 92, 101, 106

Chilcote, Paul, ix, 84, 107, 112

Christ, 3, 8, 9, 20, 21, 53, 54, 55, 62, 64, 66, 71, 72, 74, 75, 77, 78, 79, 86, 99, 100, 102, 104, 115, 116, 117, 118, 119, 121, 122, 124, 126, 130, 131
Christianity, "True," 7–16
Christianity, Wesley's view of "Essentials of," 4–7
Christmas Carol, 110
Christology, Wesley's and the affections, 74–75
1 Chronicles 28:9, 19
church, 3, 4, 6, 7, 8, 10, 12, 14, 16, 18, 20, 21, 22, 24, 26, 28, 29, 30, 34, 36, 38, 40, 42, 44, 46, 48, 50, 54, 56, 58, 60, 62, 64, 65, 66, 67, 70, 72, 74, 75, 76, 78, 80, 82, 84, 83, 85, 86, 88, 92, 94, 96, 98, 99, 100, 102, 104, 106, 108, 110, 112, 113, 114, 115, 116, 118, 120, 122, 124, 125, 126, 127, 128, 129, 130, 132
"Church's One Foundation is Jesus Christ Her Lord, The," 115
church's work seen in preaching, counseling, and evangelism, 115–30
circumcision of the heart, 24
class meetings as necessary for growth, 86, 116, 122
cognitive dimension of emotions/affections, 41–44, 47–50
Collins, Kenneth, ix, 51n, 58
Colossians 2:13, 22; 4:11, 54
Community as necessary for heart renewal, 76–83
Concluding Unscientific Postscript, 93
conscience, 22, 23, 24, 60
consolation(s), 54, 55, 57
construals, emotions/affections as, 46–47
conversion, understood as from the works of the flesh to the fruit of the Spirit, 129–30
1 Corinthians 1:24, 53; 2:3, 25; 5:8, 71; 13, 119, 121; 13:3, 97; 14:6, 26; 14:20, 25; 14:32, 26; 15:31, 11

2 Corinthians 1:3, 54; 1:12, 23, 60; 3:3, 21; 5:13, 72; 7:1, 71; 9:6, 77; 13:11, 54
Cottingham, John, 27, 47, 105
counseling, and pastoral care that shapes the heart, 120–25
creeds, 9, 14
cross, 55, 62, 78, 79, 86, 100, 101, 115, 118, 123
crying, 56, 57, 124. See also "tears"
curving in on oneself, 85

David, 21
death, 5, 8, 23, 42, 64, 102, 104, 115, 122, 123, 127
deists, 14
Deschner, John, 74, 75
despair, 65, 107, 124
Deuteronomy 2:30, 17; 30:6, 24
devil, 8, 9, 17, 27, 57, 67, 58, 125. See also "Satan"
Dickens, Charles, 110
discipleship, 86, 100, 122, 124, 125
dispositional, nature of the affections, 76–78
Dixon, Thomas, 33, 34, 35, 36, 37, 38, 42
doctrines, essential, 4–7, 99–100
"door of faith," 116, 118–19
Dreyer, Frederick, 69
Dykstra, Craig, 93

"Earnest Appeal to Men of Reason and Religion, An," 15, 104
Edwards, Jonathan, 35, 48, 69, 83, 102
emotion(s), 4, 20, 24, 25, 29, 31, 33, 34, 35, 36, 37, 38, 39, 40, 41, 42, 43, 44, 45, 46, 47, 48, 49, 50, 51, 52, 53, 55, 57, 58, 59, 61, 63, 64, 65, 66, 67, 68, 72, 73, 76, 80, 85, 87, 88, 107, 108, 109, 117, 118, 121, 126
Emotions: An Essay in Aid of Moral Psychology, 45–47
emotions, defined by Lauritzen, 49
emotions, defined by Nussbaum, 41
emotions, defined by Roberts, 45–46

emotions, vocabulary shift regarding, 34–38
Empfindung, 36
empiricism, 69
enthusiasm, 80
enthusiast(s), 26, 55, 58, 80, 85
envy, 39, 78, 82, 129
Ephesians 1:18, 53; 4:13, 53; 4:18, 69; 4:23, 22; 5:16, 54; 5:19, 21
Erdt, Terrence, 69
Eskimos, 50
ethics, 40, 45, 47
eucharist, 104
eudaemonism, 10, 11, 40, 43, 131
evangelism, Wesleyan, 125–30
evil, 18, 19, 20, 26, 62, 73, 84, 124
Exodus 4:21, 17; 7:13, 17; 8:15, 17; 8:19, 17
experience and the affections, 52–67
Explanatory Notes upon the New Testament, 10, 99
Explanatory Notes upon the Old Testament, 10, 17
expression of the affections as necessary for their existence, 78–88
Ezekiel 3:20, 18; 36:26, 19

faith as the "door of the house of religion, 116–19
faith as the handmaid to love, 14, 75
"Farther Appeal, Part I, A," 16
fear, 8, 13, 24, 25, 29, 35, 42, 43, 53, 61, 65, 76, 78, 83, 86, 101, 107, 128, 130
feelings, distinguished from emotions/affections, 52–67
Felch, Susan, 101
Feuerbach, Ludwig, 87,
Flaubert, Gustav, 106
Forrest Gump, 110, 111
foundationalism, 102, 104
freedom, 18, 98, 111, 131
Freud, Sigmund, 88
friendship, 95, 111, 119

"fruit of the Spirit," 14, 59, 108, 116, 121, 126; as the goal of the Christian life, 129, 130

Gadamer, Hans-Georg, 86
Galatians 4:17–18, 26; 5, 129–30; 5:6, 9; 5:22–24, 59, 62, 121
Geertz, Clifford, 93
Gefühl, 36
generosity, 121, 129
genesis of the affections, 68–76, 86–87
Glasson, Francis, 22, 23
God, 5, 8, 9, 10, 13, 14, 15, 17, 18, 19, 20, 21, 22, 23, 24, 26, 27, 28, 29, 34, 35, 48, 51, 53, 54, 55, 56, 58, 59, 60, 61, 62, 63, 64, 65, 66, 67, 70, 71, 72, 73, 74, 75, 76, 77, 78, 79, 80, 81, 82, 83, 85, 86, 87, 88, 95, 96, 97, 98, 102, 111, 115, 116, 117, 118, 119, 120, 121, 122, 123, 124, 125, 126, 128, 130, 131, 132
grace, 7, 8, 9, 17, 18, 22, 26, 28, 29, 51, 55, 60, 61, 79, 86, 96, 91, 111, 122, 125, 129
"grand doctrines," 4
gratitude, 13, 28, 78, 95, 96
Graver, Margaret R., 34, 35
Green, Joel, 105
Grenz, Stanley, 104
grief, 42, 43, 57
Griffiths, Paul E., 38, 46

Haartman, Keith 45
happiness, 10, 11, 13, 16, 17, 40, 60, 72, 78, 106, 131, 132
"happiness and holiness," 10, 11, 106
hate, 17, 39, 97, 124
Hauerwas, Stanley, 48, 84, 97
Hays, Richard, 105n
heart, 29, 30, 33, 35, 37, 38, 42, 44, 47n, 48, 51n, 52, 55, 56, 57, 60, 61, 64, 67, 69, 71, 73, 74, 75, 76, 78, 79, 80, 81, 82, 83, 84, 85, 86, 87, 88, 91, 92, 93, 95, 96, 97, 98, 99, 100, 101, 102, 103, 104, 105, 106, 107, 108, 109, 110, 111, 112, 113, 114,

heart (*continued*)
        115, 116, 118, 119, 120, 121, 122,
        123, 124, 125, 126, 130, 131, 132
heart, Wesley's understanding of, 3–16
heart's relations with reason, 17–28
heart renewal as Wesley's orienting
        concern, 28–30
"heart religion" as practical theology,
        91–98
heathen, 8, 26, 65, 80
heaven, 27, 60, 74, 82
Hebrews 2:3, 11; 12:11, 11
Heitzenrater, Richard, 4, 5, 12
hell, 82
Herod, 23
Holifield, Brooks, 48
holiness, 4, 5, 6, 7, 9, 10, 11, 13, 17, 29,
        66, 71, 72, 74, 75, 79, 81, 87, 93,
        94, 95, 96, 97, 98, 106, 108, 116,
        117, 118, 119, 121, 122, 131, 132
Holmer, Paul, 99
Homilies of the Church of England, 7, 99
hope, 8, 9, 10, 23, 29, 33, 42, 53, 77, 85,
        86, 109, 110,113
"house of religion," 116–20
house itself as holiness, 116, 119–20
Hume, David, 35, 36, 38
humility, 13, 14, 20, 28, 78, 80, 86, 105,
        128, 131
Hutcheson, Francis, 60

idolatry, 10, 80, 122, 129
idols, 10
"image of God", 13, 27, 51, 74, 81, 95,
        117, 125, 126, 128, 132
impulses, 18, 19, 26, 27, 36, 55, 56, 80
inner and outer aspects of affectivity,
        71–72
intellectual component of the affections,
        see "cognitive dimension of
        emotions/affections"
intentionality of emotions/affections, 42,
        43, 48, 50, 64
irrational, 18, 24, 25, 35, 36, 76
Isaiah, 6:1ff, 117

Jakes, T. D., 67
James, William, 37, 53
James 1, 55; 1:5, 25; 2:14, 76; 2:22, 77
Jeremiah 11:20, 19; 17:9, 19, 20:12, 19
Jesus, 8, 9, 11, 14, 21, 57, 66, 72, 77, 79,
        85, 97, 102, 115, 117, 118, 123,
        124
Jews/Judaism, 45, 75, 85
Job, 123
Joel, 18
John 2:2, 105; 8:9, 23; 12:36, 10; 16:12,
        26; 18:36, 71
1 John, 11, 15, 120; 1:5, 70; 3:16, 119,
        121; 3:17, 79; 3:19, 23; 4:1, 27, 79;
        4:11, 79; 4:19, 15
Jones, Greg 99
Joshua 24:16, 18
joy, 16, 29, 35, 53, 55, 57, 59, 60, 64, 65,
        66, 70, 75, 78, 79, 80, 86, 95, 100,
        101, 104, 106, 108, 110, 119, 121,
        129
Jude 1:10, 70
Judges 21:25 19
justification, 4, 5, 7, 15, 63, 74

Kant, Immanuel, 36
Keck, Leander, 75, 129
Kempis, Thomas a, 7
Kierkegaard, Søren, 93, 103, 104
Kimbrough, S. T., 104
"kingdom of God," 66, 75, 122
Knight, Henry, 48, 116

Langford, Thomas, 5
Large Minutes, 87
Lauritzen, Paul, 38, 47–51, 48, 49, 50, 51,
law, 7, 14, 19, 27, 39, 62, 63, 64, 74, 75,
        79, 80, 117, 121
Lewis, C. S., 27, 87, 119
licentiousness, 129
Lindbeck, George, 26, 93
Locke, John, 53, 69, 101
Long, D. Stephen, 83, 84
love, 8, 9, 10, 13, 14, 15, 16, 21, 24, 26,
        27, 28, 29, 34, 35, 39, 40, 44, 51,
        53, 57, 59, 60, 61, 62, 63, 65, 66,

70, 71, 73, 74, 75, 76, 77, 78, 81, 82, 83, 86, 95, 96, 97, 98, 100, 101, 104, 106, 108, 110, 112, 113, 114, 118, 119, 120, 121, 123, 124, 125, 129, 130, 131
Lowery, Kevin, 83
Lowrie, Walter, 104
Luke 1:13, 21; 2:27, 56; 3:8, 21; 4:28, 77; 9:44, 79; 10:27, 24; 11:33, 72; 11:44, 71, 97; 13:4, 124; 13:5, 117; 15:14, 54; 15:31, 71; 16, 78; 16:3, 78; 20:20, 23; 24:25, 22; 24:45, 22
Luther, Martin, 85

MacIntyre, Alisdair, 48, 76, 93
Madame Bovary, 106
Maddox, Randy, 5n, 28, 29, 38n, 51n, 58, 70n, 91, 92, 94n, 97, 98, 107n
Mark 6:26, 23; 6:52, 69; 12:33, 21
Marshall, G.D., 44, 45, 66, 67
masturbation, 85
Matthew 4:1, 57; 4:11, 56; 5:3, 12; 5:12, 12; 5:21–29, 97; 5:48, 12; 5–7, 12; 6:1, 77; 6:9, 26; 6:10n, 11; 6:21–23, 73; 6:31, 69; 7:15, 71; 7:16, 77; 13:14, 23; 13:26, 79; 14:9, 22; 16:24, 79; 18:3–4, 131; 18:15, 79; 23:6, 23; 23:27, 71
Matthews, Rex, 69n
McGinn, Bernard, 70, 73
Meredith, Lawrence, 6
Methodism/Methodist, 4, 5, 6, 7, 38, 52, 61, 74, 82, 83, 85, 86, 87, 93, 99, 109, 116, 120, 122, 125
Middleton, Conyers, 12
Miller, Perry, 69
Moravians, 62, 64
Moses, 17
Murphy, Nancey, 70, 97
Music Man, 66, 111, 112, 113
mystics, 64

Neu, Jerome, 38, 57
"new birth," 4n, 5n, 80
Niebuhr, H. Richard, 87n

Noah, 113
Nussbaum, Martha, 38, 39–45, 46, 47, 48, 49, 107, 108, 109

Object-relatedness of affections, 68–76
Occasion of an affection, vs. its cause or object, 44–45
Oord, ix,
orthodoxy, 5, 9, 92
orthokardia, 68, 92, 94n, 108,129
orthopathy, 92
orthopraxis, 92, 129
Outler, Albert, 4, 10, 12n, 13n, 27, 58, 61, 62, 63n, 125

passion(s), 18, 34, 35, 36, 37, 38, 47, 57, 62, 70, 78, 82, 94, 95, 106, 109
patience, 121, 129
Paul, 25, 56, 57, 75, 76, 97, 105, 121, 129
peace, 8, 9, 13, 14, 16, 59, 60, 64, 65, 66, 70, 75, 80, 86, 95, 100, 104, 106, 108, 121, 129
perfect/perfection, 35, 52, 62, 63, 65, 81, 82, 113
perfection and sin, 61–66
Perlez, Jane, 128
Pharaoh, 17
Philippians 1:9–10, 70; 1:10–11, 79; 2:5, 8
Philemon, 54
Philips (translation), 10
phroneite, 25
phronountes, 25
Pietism, 4
Plato, 10
pleasure, 21, 36, 54, 55, 73, 86, 110, 121
Pojman, Louis, 47, 127
Poole, Matthew, 11, 17
poor, 97, 120, 121
"porch of repentance," 116–18
porch, 5, 116, 117, 122, 131
practical theology and essential Christian doctrine, 99–100
practical theology, the heart and narrative, 107–15
prayer, 3, 19, 21, 72, 114

preaching, 62, 72, 92, 93, 94, 107, 109,
111, 113, 115, 116, 117, 118, 119,
121, 123, 125, 127, 129, 131
preaching for the renewal of the heart,
116–20
predestination, 18
prevenient grace, 18
pride, 15, 25, 39, 63, 78, 82
Proudfoot, Wayne, 47,
Proust, Marcel, 39, 41, 108
Psalms 7:9, 19; 105:25, 17

quadrilateral, 52

rage, 39
Rahner, Karl, 70
rationality, 25, 76
reason, 10, 15, 16, 22, 24, 25, 26, 27, 35,
36, 40, 47, 52, 56, 76, 83, 84, 88,
104, 105, 105, 106, 112
reason's relationship with the heart,
24–27
redemption, 9, 125
Reformation, 75
reformers, 127
Reid, Thomas, 38
relativism, 126, 127, 128
religion, "true," 12, 14, 25, 51, 71, 81, 83,
86, 95
*Religious Belief and Emotional
Transformation*, 47–51
renewal of the heart as the axial theme of
Wesley's soteriology, 27
repentance, 5, 6, 7, 9, 14, 20, 62, 63, 80,
86, 98, 116, 117, 118, 122, 131
resentment, 49, 50, 63
resurrection, 8, 72, 102, 115, 124
Revelation 2:23, 22; 3:15–16, 130
revelation(s), 56, 65
Rigg, Georgia, x
righteousness, 8, 11, 12, 22, 75, 79, 80
Roberts, Robert, ix, 38, 45–47, 48, 49, 95,
96, 105
Rogers, Charles, 18
Romans 1:4, 72; 1:21, 72; 1:25, 71; 2:29,
24; 5:5, 8; 8:5, 73; 8:16, 58; 8:27,

20; 10:2, 26; 10:10, 22; 12:15,
124; 12:16, 25
Runyon, Theodore, 92
Rutherford, Dr., 61
Ryle, Gilbert, 56

sacraments, 29, 75, 99, 116
Saliers, Don E., ix, 20, 47, 88, 103,
salvation, 3, 7, 11, 64, 74, 81, 95, 100,
101, 129
1 Samuel 16:7, 19
sanctification, 5, 63, 108, 125, 128, 130
sanctified, life as a confident witness,
129–30
Sartre, Jean Paul, 88
Satan, 17, 54, 83. See also "devil"
Sauter, Gerhard, 28
Schleiermacher, Friedrich D. E., 27, 29,
60, 75, 87, 93
Schopenhauer, Arthur, 36
Screwtape Letters, 87
Scripture, 8, 10, 11, 14, 15, 16, 17, 19, 23,
27, 33, 52, 53, 56, 57, 59, 60, 73,
79, 85, 105, 119, 123, 124, 130
Scripture and heart renewal, 17–30
Scrooge, Ebeneezer, 110
self-deception and the affections, 78–80
sensations, 6, 37, 48, 54, 58, 75
sermon on the mount, 11, 12, 81, 117
Sermons of John (and Charles) Wesley:
1, "Salvation by Faith," 8, 81
2, "The Almost Christian," 9, 61n
3, "Awake Thou That Sleepest," 61
(Charles Wesley)
4, "Scriptural Christianity," 9
5, "Justification by Faith," 15
7, "The Way to the Kingdom," 9,
81, 83n, 95
9, "Spirit of Bondage and
Adoption," 61n
10, "The Witness of the Spirit,
Discourse I," 58, 59
11, "The Witness of the Spirit,
Discourse II," 59
12, "The Witness of Our Own
Spirit," 60, 61, 61n

13, "On Sin in Believers," 62, 63

14, "The Repentance of Believers,"
63

21, "The First Discourse on the
Sermon on the Mount," 12

24, "The Fourth Discourse on the
Sermon on the Mount," 81, 82

26, "The Sixth Discourse on the
Sermon on the Mount," 81

33, "The Thirteenth Discourse on
the Sermon on the Mount," 11

36, "The Law Established by Faith,
Discourse II," 14

37, "The Nature of Enthusiasm," 80

41, "Wandering Thoughts" 63n

44, "Original Sin," 27

46, "The Wilderness State," 63n

47, "Heaviness Through Manifold
Temptations," 63n

62, "The End of Christ's Coming," 9

70, "The Case of Reason
Impartially Considered," 10

71, "Of Good Angels," 84n

74, "Of the Church," 14

76, "On Perfection," 62, 81

78, "Spiritual Idolatry," 10

87, "The Danger of Riches," 82

89, "The More Excellent Way," 9,
61n

106, "On Faith," 61n

107, "On God's Vineyard," 5

117, "On The Discoveries of Faith,"
61n

122, "Causes of the Inefficacy of
Christianity," 82

130, "On Living Without God,"
9, 10

Shaftesbury, 3rd Earl of, 60

sin, 4, 5, 7, 22, 27, 35, 45, 52, 54, 61, 62,
63, 64, 70, 71, 111, 117, 123, 124,
129

singing with your heart, 21

"sinless perfection not being Wesley's
term of choice, 62–63

"Smith, John," 83, 94

Socrates, 20

Solomon, Robert, 38, 48

sorrow, 26

soteriology, 27

soul, 20, 48, 13, 21, 24, 35, 36, 57, 60, 61,
62, 66, 72, 73, 76, 77, 81, 84, 88,
120, 121

"spiritual senses," 69–70

spirituality, 5, 45, 70, 73, 94, 104, 126

Staples, Jenna, ix

Steele, Richard, 48, 83, 93, 96, 97

Steinbeck, John, 49

Stendahl, Krister, 75

Stoics, 34, 35, 41, 54

supernatural, 26, 80

synergism, 75

teaching, 98, 99, 103

teaching for the renewal of the heart,
91–106

tears, 57, 118. See also "crying"

telos (end or goal), 62, 68, 69, 71, 73, 75,
76, 77, 79, 81, 83, 85, 87, 122,
132

"temper" (affection), 13, 21, 35, 51, 55,
57, 58, 62, 74, 77, 79, 82, 84, 95

temptation(s), 57, 63, 87, 96, 123

Teresa, Mother, 120

thankfulness, 11, 72, 82, 96

theology, 4, 5, 6, 12, 13, 15, 16, 18, 28,
29, 33, 38, 40, 56, 63, 68, 69, 76,
84, 91, 92, 93, 97, 98, 99, 100,
101, 102, 103,104, 105, 106, 107,
108, 116, 129, 130

theology and spirituality, inseparability
of, 101–6

theology, heart religion as practical,
91–99

1 Thessalonians 2:17, 57, 77; 4:6, 26; 5:21,
27, 79

Thompson, E. P., 85

Titus 2:4, 26

tradition, 6, 7, 37, 41, 52, 70, 73, 74, 83,
84, 91, 92, 93, 94, 99, 101, 103,
104, 105, 106, 108, 112, 113, 114,
115, 116, 124, 125, 126, 128

tragedy, heart formation after, 123–25

transitivity of affectivity, 64, 72, 73
Trinity, 6, 67, 99, 100, 101, 102, 104
trivium, 103
Tyson, J. H., ix
Tyson, John R., 98

Uganda, 128
Upheavals of Thought, 39–45
Utku (Eskimos), 50, 128

vocation, 14, 102, 116
Volf, Miroslav, 93, 99,
voluntarism/voluntarist, 83, 84
von Balthasar, Hans Urs, 70

Wainwright, William, 22, 47, 105
Wainwright, Geoffrey, 75
warmed heart, 64
Watson, David Lowes, 86, 122
Wesley, Charles, 6, 61, 65, 84
Wesley, Emilia, 82
Wesley, John, 3, 4, 5, 6, 7, 8, 10, 11, 12,
        13, 14, 15, 16, 17, 18, 19, 20, 21,
        22, 23, 24, 25, 26, 27, 28, 29, 30,
        33, 34, 35, 37, 38, 39, 40, 44, 45,
        48, 51, 52, 53, 54,55, 56, 57, 58,
        59, 60, 61, 62, 63, 64, 65, 66, 67,
        68, 69, 70, 71, 72, 73, 74, 75, 76,
        77, 78, 79, 80, 81, 82, 83, 84, 85,
        86, 87, 88, 91, 92, 93, 94, 95, 96,
        97, 98, 99, 100, 101, 102, 103,
        104, 105, 106, 107, 108, 109, 116,
        117, 118, 119, 120, 121, 122, 125,
        129, 130, 131, 132
Whitefield, George, 4, 5
Wittgenstein, Ludwig, 88, 93, 99
works and the heart, 80–87
works of mercy, 86
works of piety, 122
worship, 21, 67, 71, 81, 83, 103, 109, 115
wounds, 124, 125
Wright, N. T., 14
Wuthnow, Robert, 94
Wynn, Mark R., 47, 105

zeal, 26, 51, 78
Zechariah 2:7, 18
zoe, 27